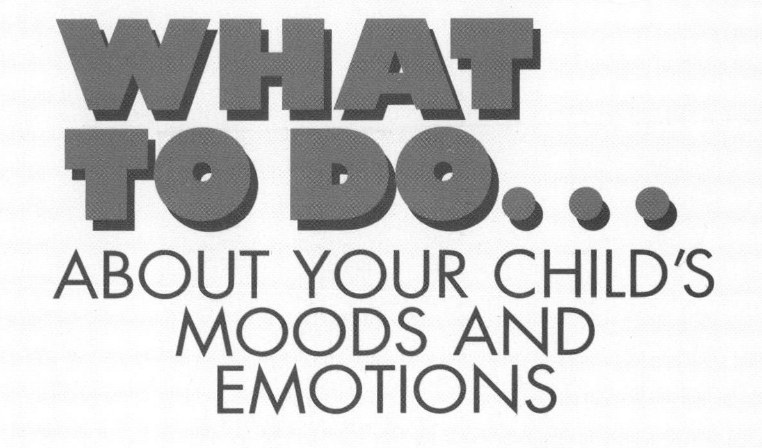
WHAT
TO DO...
ABOUT YOUR CHILD'S
MOODS AND
EMOTIONS

WHAT TO DO...

ABOUT YOUR CHILD'S MOODS AND EMOTIONS

ROBERTA ISRAELOFF

The Reader's Digest Association, Inc.
Pleasantville, N.Y./Montreal

About the Author

Roberta Israeloff has been a contributing editor of *Parents'* magazine for over six years. She also writes regularly on family and psychological issues for other national magazines, including *Good Housekeeping, Family Circle, Woman's Day,* and *The New York Times*, and is the author and co-author of five books. The most recent is the forthcoming *Kindling the Flame*. She lives on Long Island with her husband and two sons, ages 10 and 16.

Consultant Justine McCabe, Ph.D., is a child psychologist in private practice in New Milford, Connecticut. She has worked at the Institute for Living in Hartford, the Waterbury Child Guidance Clinic, and the New Milford Mental Health Clinic.

Acknowledgments

I'd like to thank the many parents and children interviewed in these pages who so thoughtfully and candidly examined their rich emotional lives, figuring out what makes them feel the way they do, and how they handle these feelings. In all cases, their names have been changed to protect their privacy. Many psychologists were also exceedingly generous with their time and insights, and I thank them all as well, particularly Drs. Stella Chess, Rebecca Eder, Susan Heitler, Michael Lewis, Carol Moog, Patricia Owen, Carolyn Saarni, and Janice Zeman. Finally, I'm grateful, as I always am, to Lynn Seligman and Ellen Ostrow, and to David, Ben, and Jacob—for everything.

A Reader's Digest Book

Conceived, written, and produced by Pen & Pencil Books.
Reader's Digest Parenting Guide Series creators:
Elin McCoy (editorial); Judy Speicher (design)

Cover photograph: Pascal Crapet/Tony Stone Images
Photographs: 7 Chip Henderson/Tony Stone Images, 13 Tony Freeman/PhotoEdit, 18 Ian Shaw/Tony Stone Images, 23 Barbara Peacock/FPG International LLC, 24 Joe McBride/Tony Stone Images, 27 Penny Tweedie/Tony Stone Images, 31 Myrleen Ferguson/PhotoEdit, 32 Jeff Greenberg/PhotoEdit, 38 Lawrence Migdale/Tony Stone Images, 41 Jennie Woodcock/Tony Stone Images, 44 Robert Brenner/PhotoEdit, 50 Pascal Crapet/Tony Stone Images, 55 David Young-Wolf/PhotoEdit, 61 Tony Freeman/PhotoEdit, 64 Rosanne Olson/Tony Stone Images, 73 Scott Barrow Inc./stock Barrow, 76 Laura Dwight/PhotoEdit, 79 Barbara Filet/Tony Stone Images, 81 Robert Brenner/PhotoEdit, 82 Tony Freeman/PhotoEdit, 85 Tony Freeman/PhotoEdit, 87 Telegraph Colour Library/FPG International LLC, 91 Gerhard Steiner/Masterfile.

Library of Congress Cataloging in Publication Data
Israeloff, Roberta. 1952-
What to do… about your child's moods and emotions / Roberta Israeloff.
p. cm. — (Reader's Digest parenting guides)
ISBN 0-7621-0100-8
1. Emotions in children. 2. Child rearing. I. Title. II. Series.
BF723.E6I87 1998
649' .1—dc21 98-5415

Printed in the United States of America

CONTENTS

Between the ages of five and thirteen, children become more aware of their feelings and learn to express them in ways that are acceptable to their parents, siblings, friends, and teachers. In other words, they learn—we hope—to become "emotionally intelligent." As parents rapidly discover, however, kids don't develop these abilities in a smooth, systematic way. All are moody and have trouble handling their emotions from time to time, both at home and at school.

We often worry when our children explode in anger, are afraid of going to bed, or suddenly turn moody. Many of us aren't sure how to help kids handle their negative emotions—or how to encourage positive ones—and we ask ourselves questions like these:

Why is Michael afraid of the dark? What will make him feel safe?

How can I get Janet to stop worrying that no one likes her?

Do Andy's blue moods mean he's depressed?

What will boost Ellen's self-esteem when she's convinced she's a failure?

What makes Lisa grumpy? Can I help her to be more cheerful?

For most parents, dealing with our kids' moods and emotions—and helping them learn to, as well—is difficult. But it's an essential part of parenting because having "emotional intelligence" contributes to success and happiness in life.

That's what this book is about.

The first section, **Real Stories & Situations,** is filled with stories of real children ages five to thirteen and the typical problems that arise as a result of their moods and emotions. In **Understanding The Problem,** you'll find answers to basic questions parents ask about the emotions kids have, from what makes them angry to why middle-school kids are moody. **What To Do** offers sound, practical solutions—actions that will help you help your children learn to manage feelings of anger, sadness, fear, jealousy, and more. The fourth section, **Year By Year,** is a quick reference to how kids' emotions change with age. **We Recommend** lists the best books, games, cassette tapes, and videos on the subject to share with your children, and resources to further your own understanding.

REAL STORIES & SITUATIONS

Is One Of These Your Child's Story?

Daniel, Age 5

Every night for the past two weeks Daniel has begged his mom at bedtime, "Check the closet again."

"I've checked it twice!" she always says.

"Did you look under the bed, too?"

"Yes," she replies. "And in all the dresser drawers. And behind the curtains. There are no spiders *anywhere* in your room."

"You can't be sure," Daniel warns, a frightened look on his face. "They crawl in and hide so you can't always see them."

Daniel's fear of spiders seemed to have come out of the blue. One night he'd spied a daddy longlegs in the corner of the bathroom and let out a cry of terror. Even after his dad put it outside, Daniel was still worried, sure another one would turn up. His parents were surprised. Dan had always been fascinated by creatures of all kinds.

To help him get over his fear, they brought home library books about insects to appeal to the budding scientist in Dan and stories about kids who learned *not* to be afraid of monsters. But although Daniel enjoyed these, when he climbed into bed his fear of spiders started all over again.

"Maybe we should call the pediatrician," Dan's dad finally suggested. "We don't want this to turn into some kind of phobia."

"I wonder if he's really afraid of spiders," Daniel's mom mused, "or if he can't say what's really scaring him." But Dan claimed he wasn't scared of anything else.

Jessica, Age 6

For her sixth birthday party, Jessica and her five best friends spent an hour at a local beauty salon where they had their nails painted and their hair styled. Then, laughing, they all headed to Jessica's house for cake and gift-opening. But the minute they walked in the door, Jessica, barely able to contain herself, insisted, "I want to open my presents right now!"

The first one was a makeup kit. "How nice!" Jessica's mother exclaimed.

"I already have one," Jessica pouted.

"It's still a very nice present. I'm sure you want to say thank you to Marie."

Jessica glared at Marie but didn't say anything. Instead, she pulled the wrapping paper off two more, looked at each one, and then put them aside.

"Take it easy," her dad said. "You need to say thank you as you go along."

"I'm not saying thank you for this junk," Jessica cried. "Annie got ten times better presents at her party. These toys are all yucky." Then she began crying furiously, just like a two-year-old having a temper tantrum.

Her dad said sternly, "Jessica! Stop this!" but his words seemed to enrage her even more. Her parents wanted to say something to Jessica's puzzled and hurt friends but didn't know where to begin. They wondered: aren't six-year-olds too old to have temper tantrums?

MATTHEW, AGE 7

Linda sat down on the comfy loveseat in the family room next to her three-year-old son, Andrew, and started reading aloud his favorite book, *Cowboy Small*. His older brother, Matthew, who had been playing happily with his Legos in the corner, suddenly insisted on squeezing in next to them, and then announced in a loud, disgusted voice, "This is a baby book."

"This is the book Andrew wants to hear," his mom replied, "and it's his story time. You can be here, too, but you have to listen quietly."

"Okay," Matt said, but within a couple of minutes he began singing a song.

"Tell him to stop," Andrew insisted.

"I won't!" Matthew said, snuggling up to Linda and jabbing his brother.

"Go away," whined Andrew.

This sort of situation had been happening a lot recently, and Linda didn't know what to do about it. Matt seemed to grow more jealous of his brother every day. Yet she remembered that he hadn't acted terribly upset when Andrew was born and had generally been very good about sharing toys with him. Now Matt was possessive about everything—his toys, his time with his parents, even his friends. Group play-dates with several friends left him in tears.

What's making him jealous now? Linda wondered. And what can I say to Matt to help him feel more secure?

LISA, AGE 8

Seven AM. Annette Marshall has to wake her daughter, Lisa, for school and she dreads it. Lisa has always been difficult in the morning, but over the past three months she has become grouchier than ever. Mornings in the Marshall house are frequently unpleasant for everyone, and Lisa is the reason. Her younger sister calls Lisa "The Grump."

Getting Lisa out of bed is just the beginning of the struggle. Her parents have tried alarm clocks with loud buzzers and with music, and they've even made Lisa go to bed a half an hour earlier. Now they shake her shoulder and steel themselves when she gets mad and yells, "Go away!"

Lisa's morning mood translates into complaints about every part of getting ready for school, from washing her face ("The washcloth is too rough. The water is too hot.") to getting dressed ("I hate these pants. I have nothing to wear.") to eating breakfast ("There's too much syrup on these waffles. The orange juice tastes bad."). When her parents try to joke her out of her mood, she doesn't crack a smile.

To ease morning tensions, Annette suggested Lisa choose her clothes and breakfast menu and pack her backpack the night before, but that hasn't helped her mood. By the time Lisa gets on the school bus, Annette is furious, exhausted, and feels like crawling back into bed.

ASK THE EXPERTS

When your child is very emotional—whether angry, sad, or afraid—psychologists advise:

- **Listen carefully first. Try to figure out what feelings lie beneath your child's words and actions.**
- **Don't just assume that you know what your child is feeling. Ask a few questions to be sure you understand.**
- **Stay calm and don't overreact.**
- **Accept your child's feelings—whatever they are—as normal.**
- **Let your child try to fix the problem.**

MICKEY, AGE 9

School had always been very easy for self-confident, good-natured Mickey. He learned quickly, enjoyed being with his classmates, and got along well with his teachers. Fourth grade began on an especially promising and exciting note: he was finally old enough to work on the school newspaper and join the science club.

Within a month, though, his feelings about school took a nose dive. He seemed consumed with self-pity and frustration: there were too many tests, too much homework, and the work was too hard. When seven PM rolled around and Mickey sat down at his desk to begin his math, things never went smoothly. He'd work industriously until he came to a tough problem he couldn't solve easily. At that point he would put down his pencil and slam his book shut. "This is too much work," he would exclaim to his dad. "Look at this, two whole pages of problems. I can't do them. I'll never finish. I'm going to get a zero in math."

Mickey's dad advised, "Take one problem at a time and stick with it," and suggested scheduling some extra homework time after school so he could get the work done, but that just resulted in an argument. Mickey wouldn't listen and was more frustrated than ever.

MEGAN, AGE 10

"My mom is my best friend," Megan had written in her journal. "I can tell her almost anything."

Jeannie, Megan's mom, closed the book, and looked into her daughter's expectant face. She had so many feelings that she wasn't sure where to begin—and Megan was standing right beside her, awaiting her reaction.

"This is a lovely tribute," she began, "and I'll treasure it all my life." She reached for Megan's hand. It was true—they had

PARENT TIPS

Check Your Own Reaction

- Jessica's dad, Frank, was embarrassed by his daughter's public temper tantrum. "I realized that I wasn't trying to figure out why she felt so upset," he says. "I needed to block out the fact that other people were around and just focus on her. When she's having an emotional meltdown like that, she needs me more than ever."
- Megan's mom, Jeannie, was convinced that her daughter's emotional reaction was unique and didn't talk about her worries to anyone. When she finally broached the subject to a friend, she felt very relieved. "As it turns out, my daughter wasn't the only one who felt this way," she says. "Just knowing that reassured me tremendously."
- Stephanie's mom, Joan, kept trying to do something about her daughter's hurt feelings. "Finally I realized she didn't expect me to wave a magic wand and make her feel better," says Joan. "She just wanted me to listen to her and empathize."

always been very close. Megan told her mother all about her friends and the fights she had with them, and shared her concerns about school. When Megan had slept over at a friend's house recently, she'd even left a note saying "I love you" under her mother's pillow.

Lately Jeannie had begun to wonder if it was normal for her daughter to act so loving toward her. Jeannie's friends frequently complained that *their* preteen daughters now seemed to be angry with them much of the time. They described daily struggles over just about everything—makeup, clothes, bedtimes, privacy. Megan was different. She usually rushed to patch up quarrels that arose.

Was it possible for a daughter to act too loving to her mother? Was Megan too compliant, too accommodating?

CHARLES, AGE 11

"But what happens if I can't find my locker? What if I can't remember my lock combination?" Charles asked his dad. It was the night before the first day of middle school, and Charles was so worried he couldn't sleep.

His dad tried to reassure him. "You've visited the school already, so you know where your locker is. Your lock combination is on the inside cover of your assignment book, right where you wrote it. And if you need help, you can always ask a teacher or go to the school office."

"I'll never remember my schedule," Charles went on, as if he hadn't heard a word his father had said.

Charles' dad wasn't too concerned that his son was worried about beginning a new school, but he wished he could be of more help. Charles had been an anxious child from an early age, slow to make even small transitions, to try new things, and to take on new challenges. He usually expected the worst to happen and then was pleasantly surprised when it didn't.

"I remember that you were worried before the first day of kindergarten, too," his dad continued, trying a new tack. "Back then your elementary school seemed as unfamiliar and as scary to you as the middle school seems now. Remember?"

"That was so long ago," Charles said. "I was a baby then."

"Then think of it this way," his father offered. "By three o'clock tomorrow afternoon it will all be over. Anyway, what's the worst that can happen?"

"You don't understand," Charles said to his dad. "Anything can happen. I'm going to have a horrible day, I just know it."

ZOE, AGE 12

Zoe had always been very close to her grandmother, but when the older woman suddenly developed pneumonia and died three weeks later, Zoe didn't appear sad, grief-stricken, or even upset. She didn't cry when her mom tenderly told her about her grandma, and she didn't want to attend the funeral. Zoe's mom, Rose, wondered whether this was normal.

But six months later, Zoe was spending a lot of time brooding in her room, sifting through the jewelry box her grandmother had given her years before. Inside were a pair of old leather gloves, a beaded evening bag, and a few strands of colored beads.

"I know you miss Nana," her mother said, commiserating. "Sometimes it helps to talk about how you're feeling."

Zoe shrugged. "I don't know what to say."

"Well," her mom began, "sometimes I feel sad and lonely without Nana, and sometimes I'm angry she left us."

Zoe shrugged again. "I'm not angry," she insisted. "I just miss her."

As weeks went by, Rose noticed that Zoe was becoming more withdrawn, content to sit in her room instead of inviting friends over. When Rose went in to say goodnight, she occasionally found her daughter in tears. "I wonder where Nana is," Zoe would say. "I wish I could see her. I wish she could see me."

Now Rose was worried that Zoe was *too* grief-stricken. Was she becoming depressed? How long should she wait before talking to someone about her daughter? Whom should she talk to?

STEPHANIE, AGE 13

Stephanie arrived home from school about the same time her mom, Joan, got home from work. Usually she had a snack, talked to her mom, and then phoned her best friend. But not today. She dropped her backpack in the kitchen and dragged herself up to her room, closing the door behind her.

"Want a snack?" her mother called up.

"I don't want anything," Stephanie said in a hurt voice. "Just leave me alone."

A few minutes later Joan went up to ask what was wrong.

"Lindsay betrayed me," Stephanie blurted out, as if she didn't want to confide in her mother but couldn't help herself. "She said that she couldn't go with me to the dance on Friday night because she had to go somewhere with her parents, but she's really having some kids over to her house, and she didn't ask me. I never want to see her again in my entire life."

Joan couldn't remember when she'd seen her daughter so deeply hurt. She wanted to do a million things at once—to agree that Lindsay was horrible, to find some way to help Stephanie feel better. She started to make suggestions: "Maybe you could go with someone else to the dance. Maybe *you'd* like to have some friends over. Or we could go to the movies."

But Stephanie said, "Mom, you just don't understand." ❑

UNDERSTANDING THE PROBLEM

Answers To Basic Questions

What Moods & Emotions Do Kids Have?

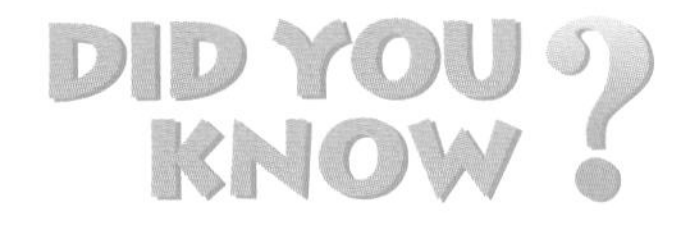

◆ The olfactory nerve (which enables us to smell) and the amygdala (two almond-shaped structures near the brainstem) are considered the "seat" or source of our emotions.

◆ Researchers have found that being aware of and able to handle emotions and moods—which they call "emotional intelligence"—contribute to a person's success and happiness in all aspects of life, including family relationships.

If you look around one morning at a school bus stop, you can't help but notice a whole range of moods and emotions in the kids waiting for the bus.

Today eight-year-old Sarah, full of smiles and chatter, waits eagerly and happily with her friend Melanie. Five-year-old Mike seems on the verge of tears as he clings to his mom with a last hug. One fourth grader frowns as he paws through his backpack at the last minute, probably worried he left a report on snails and his clean gym sweat-pants on the kitchen table. Anita's younger brother has just deliberately stepped on her new shoes, and, furious, she shrieks, "I hate you!" As a runner dashes by with his panting German shepherd, tiny Katie shrinks back fearfully, hiding behind her mom until the dog is gone.

One child is still grumpy because she "got up on the wrong side of bed" while her older brother exudes calm, in contrast to his whiny mood at the breakfast table only half an hour before.

As most parents quickly learn, the moods and emotions our kids feel are as varied as the colors in a huge box of crayons. Sometimes a child is sunny one moment and grumpy the next for no apparent reason, while at other times a blue mood hangs on for days. Some of our kids seem to feel everything intensely, while others appear almost unaffected by the same events. Sometimes we know how our kids are feeling and why—and sometimes we're mystified.

But if we understand the kinds of moods and emotions all children have and what causes them, we can help our kids learn how to master their emotions instead of feeling overwhelmed.

Emotions are natural

Feelings bubble up within our kids (and us) spontaneously, often in reaction to something specific—a kind face, being teased, the first day of school, failing a test, a jab to the stomach. They usually impel our kids (and us) to outward expression. When Annie is happy, for example, she expresses it by bursting into song or laughing. But sometimes that expression can cause trouble, as it did for Robbie. He was so angry at Tony for calling him a "dork" that he punched Tony and landed in the principal's office.

The four basic emotions

We know what emotions feel like, but they're hard to define. Many researchers believe there are four basic feelings—anger, fear, sadness, and happiness—that are universal, present in all human beings from the time they are born. (Some researchers include surprise and disgust as well.) Just as the colors we see are variations of the primary colors, so too our emotions are blends of these basic feelings.

In our kids, as in ourselves, these emotions are accompanied by different and distinct physical reactions, like a racing pulse, a hollowness in the pit of the stomach, sweatiness, or relaxed muscles. Certain facial expressions accompany them, too, and a California psychologist, Paul Ekman, has found that people from many different cultures around the world have no trouble recognizing what they mean.

With age, kids' emotions become more complex

Between the ages of five and thirteen a child's emotional palette expands to include what one researcher calls "blended" emotions. An eight-year-old's jealousy of her older sister, for example, is actually a mixture of several different basic feelings—anger, sadness, and fear. A child being teased feels angry at the teaser, but also hurt and fearful of what else the teaser may say or do. That's one reason it's sometimes hard to sort out just what kids feel.

As children become more aware of themselves, they also begin to experience self-conscious feelings like shame, envy, embarrassment, pride, and guilt. Take five-year-old Johnny. He lost his friend Sebastian's favorite action figure and claimed he didn't. Later, he felt guilty because he was old enough to be able to think about what he did and realize that what he should have done was tell the truth.

Attending school adds a dizzying world of situations that call forth complicated emotions. On a daily basis, as kids navigate their way through friendships, cliques, academic work, and sports, they have to learn to grapple with feelings of resentment, frustration, pride, and disappointment. Sometimes they have a hard time doing this without help from us. As they become older, they become increasingly anxious about their performance in school.

Gradually, starting at age nine or ten, children also come to recognize that there are degrees of intensity to emotions. Being irritated at mom for refusing to go to the mall is not as strong a feeling as fury at a friend who doesn't invite you to a party.

One of the hallmarks of adolescence is the ability to feel more than one emotion at a time, especially those that conflict. Kids still love their parents, but also fight with them; they claim to despise a teacher, but secretly admire him. At the same time they are also discovering that feelings have nuances—the love they feel for mom and dad is different from what they feel for friends, music idols, or a girl- or boyfriend. No wonder preteens' ambivalent emotions and moods often bewilder them as much as they do their parents!

Good vs. bad emotions

Most of us think of emotions and moods in terms of good and bad. We usually don't

ADVICE FROM KIDS

- Meg, 7, says, "I get:
  - angry when my sister socks me."
  - afraid of the haunted house at our school Halloween party."
- John, 10, says, "I feel:
  - mad when my parents yell at me for something I didn't do."
  - frustrated if I can't beat a video game."
- Ellen, 13, says, "I'm:
  - hurt when I know people are talking about me behind my back."
  - frustrated when teachers expect me to know something they never taught."

Psychologists agree it's important to understand the difference among feelings, thoughts, and actions. They say:

- **What we *think* about our feelings can be changed. When Aaron, didn't get the part he wanted in the class play, he thought, "I didn't get a good role so I must not be a good actor. I guess I'm just a failure." This thought can be examined and modified.**
- **We can also change what we *do* as a result of our feelings and thoughts. If a child is angry, for example, he or she can say so instead of hitting.**

worry when our kids are happy, cheerful, and in a good or positive mood. That's how we wish they could feel all the time! Life would be so much easier and more pleasant for them and for us.

It's our kids' bad, negative, or difficult emotions and moods that so often worry and upset us. But the truth is that all kids experience these at some time or another because they're a natural and healthy reaction to the normal griefs, changes, and disappointments that are a part of growing up. Grandparents die, best friends move away, brothers scribble on treasured baseball mitts, a classmate gets the part in the play that your child wanted. In response, our children may cry bitterly, storm off and sulk, kick a sibling, or act in other ways we don't find acceptable.

Sometimes bad feelings in our kids are a response to changes that pose new challenges. Think of how children often become moody or flare up with anger over nothing when they are starting school or attending a first boy-girl dance. Change is a little scary for everyone. At the same time kids believe they'll be up to it, they also worry that they won't.

All parents know that helpless feeling that comes over us when our kids are angry, miserable, disappointed, or in the throes of some other uncomfortable emotion. How we want to, and often do, say, "Cheer up. Don't feel upset." Or "There's no reason to be afraid." Yet psychologists say that kids whose parents don't allow them to have these bad emotions will eventually come to view all their feelings, even positive ones, as suspect. Surprisingly, the darker emotions like anger and jealousy that usually cause the most problems may be the ones that teach our kids the most.

Emotions can be scary

Parents often don't realize that for five- and six-year-olds, emotions can be frightening because they can be so intense, and this makes kids feel out of control. When five-year-old Tim becomes enraged because he doesn't get his way, he feels like he's going to explode—and he doesn't always remember that he'll feel calmer in a few minutes. Young kids like Tim are also convinced that just having a feeling can cause something to happen. When Tim was angry at Todd and then Todd fell and hurt himself, Tim was sure he'd caused that to happen.

Moody preteens often become upset when they don't understand or feel able to control the swings of their emotions. They start wondering why a particular boy or girl makes them happy one moment, but miserable the next.

How kids learn about feelings

Our kids learn their biggest lessons about feelings from us, starting at birth. I remember standing shoulder to shoulder with my husband watching our then week-old son fuss in his crib. "He looks so sad," my husband said. "I wish we knew what was bothering him." We wrinkled our brows and turned our lips down, becoming mirrors of his face. Imitating your child's expression and reflecting his feelings back to him, as we did, turns out to be an essential part of how our kids become aware of their own feelings.

Another essential, supplying words to describe the emotions kids are feeling, helps them associate a feeling with a word. Without a name for a feeling, it remains locked up inside them. Matt, for example, didn't know that he was feeling guilty over swiping a candy bar from his sister's room until his mom took the time to tell him that the uneasy, unhappy feeling he had was called "guilt." As many psychologists have pointed out, kids can't master their emotions unless they can recognize them.

Controlling emotions

Part of growing up in any society is understanding how to express feelings in appropriate and acceptable ways, which really means letting people know how we feel without acting in ways that hurt them or ourselves. Learning how to do this is a slow process, one that some children find more difficult than others do.

Our kids learn how to handle their moods and emotions in three main ways: through experimenting with emotional outbursts, such as tantrums; by talking about how they feel and what it makes them want to do; and from studying how we, their parents, express and handle ours. Even with our help kids rarely master their emotions in an even, systematic way—and that's one reason their emotions and moods can cause so many problems at home, at school, and with friends.

Think about your own emotions

Like most parents, I often feel as if I'm walking on a tightrope when it comes to my two sons' moods and emotions. On the one hand, I want them to explore all their feelings. I don't want them to think that only good emotions, like happiness and gratitude, are okay. On the other hand, sometimes I'm not happy with the way they're expressing those other emotions!

In order to help our kids sort out their emotions and moods, I've found that we have to look at our own. Which ones are we comfortable with and which ones cause us distress or embarrassment? Do we consider feelings a luxury, or think of them as the building-blocks of personality? Do we try to understand how and why we reacted in a particular way or do we push feelings down if they become too intense?

We can't understand or help our kids deal with their moods and emotions without attending to ours at the same time. ❑

DID YOU KNOW?

◆ A national study of children ages 7 to 16 compared their emotional well-being in the mid-1970s and at the end of the 1980s. It found a decline in kids' emotional skills and an increase in their emotional problems. At the end of the 1980s, children had more worries and fears, reported feeling more unhappy, and were more anxious and depressed, moodier, and more hot-tempered.

Many psychologists attribute this to the instability of families today and the hectic, rushed quality of family life.

Do Kids Express Their Feelings In The Same Ways?

The short answer is no. Even though all kids *experience* the same types of emotions, how they *express* them varies greatly. Just take the way the three kids in the Cohen family reacted when their beloved cat, Greta, died after she was hit by a car. Dramatic ten-year-old Allie sobbed as though her heart would break, wailing, "Why did it have to happen?" Her younger brother, Harry, blamed the driver of the car, announcing at dinner, "I wish I could punch that guy." Their older brother, Jamie, slouched up to his room to be alone.

All the Cohen kids were sad, but they each showed sadness in a different way.

It's true that kids and adults have the same physiological reactions to a particular feeling. When we're angry, as Harry was, for example, our heartbeat speeds up and our bodies pump out adrenalin to prime us to act against a foe.

But beyond instinctive reactions, the ways our children show us their emotions are as individual as fingerprints. Their feelings may show on their faces, in their body language, through the words they use, the actions they take, or any combination or all of the above. One child swears loudly and slams doors when he's angry, another gets into legalistic arguments with her parents, still another slugs his brother. Part of the difference can be laid at the door of inborn temperament (see pages 20-21), but there are several other reasons.

How age matters

Up until the age of seven, most kids are pretty direct in showing what they're feeling because they're only beginning to learn self-control. When they're angry or afraid, for example, we usually know it. Six-year-old Joe is quick to lash out with a kick or nasty name if his little brother makes him mad. But he's liable to act like a solicitous big brother fifteen minutes

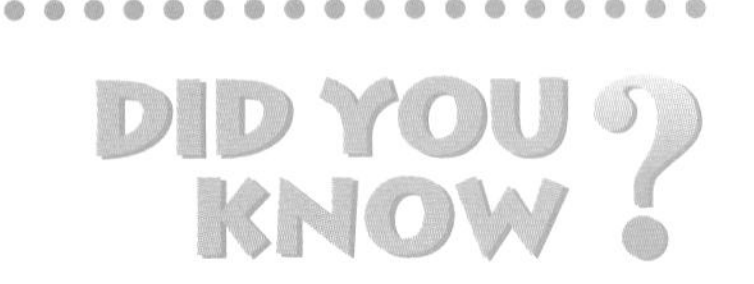

◆ According to psychologist Paul Ekman, people use between 1,000 and 3,000 facial expressions, depending on how they feel. To indicate all the different shadings of our emotions, we move and position our eyebrows and lips, open and close our eyes, and flare our nostrils.

later, because at this age kids go from one feeling to another amazingly quickly.

By the age of eight most children have developed much more self-control, so their reactions are more complex. Sometimes, in fact, they disguise what they're really feeling. Mandy, who sulks and whines a lot, may be angry—but underneath it, she may also be depressed. That's why we often have to become detectives to figure out what our kids are feeling (pages 42-43).

Boys and girls differ

In our culture girls are more likely to show their feelings—especially feelings of hurt, fear, and guilt—than boys are. The differences in the way the Cohen kids reacted are typical. At five or even six years of age both boys and girls cry when hurt, but as they go through elementary school, boys' faces reveal less and less, girls' more and more. Parents unconsciously aid and abet this. Sandra Cohen, like many parents, talks more about emotions to Allie than to her brothers. The exception is anger. Boys don't experience this emotion more than girls, but as they grow older, they show it more openly than girls in words and actions.

What they express depends . . .

Few parents will be surprised to hear that children of all ages are more likely to express how they feel to parents than to a friend or teacher. (Girls in the seventh and eighth grades, though, will confide some emotions only to their best friends!) Kids begin to control emotions depending on what they're feeling and who they're with as early as first grade. Since it's not "cool" to cry at school, they'll hold in those tears until they get home. Kids are also more likely to express some emotions than others. To most people, pain is a more acceptable emotion than anger and sadness. Some kids complain frequently about aches and pains because they know they'll get more sympathy and support from their parents than they will if they act angry.

Both cultural differences and family style have an impact, too. In Janie's family, crying is gently discouraged. When she comes home from school in tears because of a fight with her best friend, her mom says, "Go dry your eyes, then we'll talk." Anticipating this, Janie will eventually learn to hold in her tears when confiding hurt or sadness to her mom. Molly's mom, on the other hand, cries freely, especially at sad movies. So when Molly feels sad or upset, her mom almost expects her to cry.

Kids need to express feelings

Like adults, children are often strengthened by expressing their feelings to someone who cares about them. Part of our job as parents is to teach kids how to express their feelings in ways that are acceptable in the society in which they grow up. ❑

AGE FACTOR

In a study of 1st, 3rd, and 5th graders, Drs. Janice Zeman and Judy Garber found that when it comes to expressing feelings—

- First graders are equally likely to approach their moms as their dads.
- By 5th grade most children believe that fathers are less accepting of emotional displays than moms are, and seek out their mothers to talk to about their feelings.

Does Temperament Affect Kids' Moods & Emotions?

One of the biggest reasons kids, even those in the same family, vary so much in the way they experience and express emotions is their inborn temperament. Rachel, the oldest daughter in the Linz family, is fairly calm, like her mom. Not much angers or upsets her—except being teased about the boy she currently likes. Her younger sister, Ruth, is hot-tempered and often reacts intensely to situations, the way her dad does, and the family is used to the way she dramatizes. At the first snowfall, for example, she's elated, crowing with delight. The downside is that she rapidly becomes furious over something that wouldn't even faze Rachel. Frank, the middle child, vacillates between the two, taking a bit from the emotional temperament of each parent.

To help our kids understand and cope with their emotions and moods, we have to take their temperaments into account.

How temperament, mood, and emotion differ

I like to compare temperament, mood, and emotion to the weather. Temperament is like the natural climate of a region. Just as the Mohave Desert is dry, and the Pacific Northwest is rainy, so too a child's temperament is a style of behavior, a way of reacting to the world that is basically stable over time. When we say, "Sean is so excitable" or "Melinda just has a gloomy take on life," what we're talking about is temperament. This aspect of a child's personality is something he or she is born with.

Emotions are like unexpected thunderstorms or beautiful sunsets—they appear with varying intensities, last for a short time, and fade away. The younger the child, the more fleeting the feeling.

Moods are more like a heatwave or rainy spell, which shows up one day and sticks around, often outstaying its welcome. Sometimes a bad mood is sparked by a feeling of sadness or disappointment that doesn't break up and scatter but lingers—for a day, a couple of days, or even a

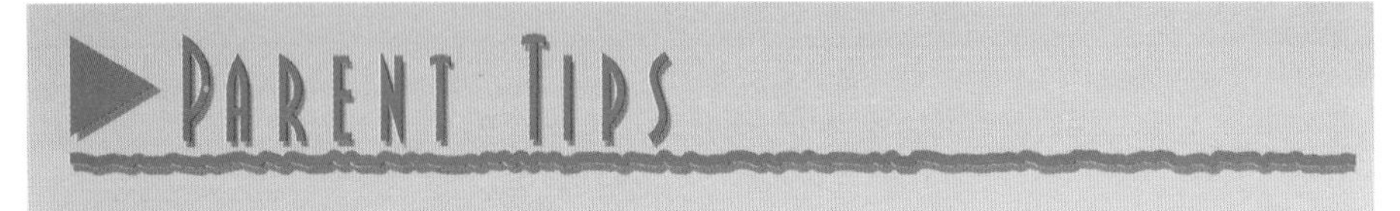

▸ ***If your child is hard to distract:***
"Instead of trying to distract my daughter from a mood, I say, 'Take ten minutes to feel bad (or sad), and then come down to the kitchen for a snack,'" explains Tina, mother of an 8-year-old girl.

▸ ***If your child has a very negative take on life:***
"When my son whines and becomes critical, I remind myself that's just how he is and ignore it the best I can. I no longer spend time feeling guilty that nothing pleases him," reports Jerry, father of a 12-year-old boy.

▸ ***If your child is very sensitive:***
"Don't assume your child is just being a grump if she complains about a shirt or bed sheets. Find out what fabrics and clothing fasteners are less irritating to her," advises Ellen, mother of 6-year-old girl.

week. Again, the younger the child, the more short-lived the mood.

It's easy to see that kids who are basically gloomy may have more blue moods than those whose personal "climate" is sunny.

The anatomy of temperament

The pioneers in studying kids and temperament, psychiatrists Stella Chess and Alexander Thomas, identified nine basic traits. Each covers a spectrum from low to high, and where children fit on it affects how they feel and express emotions. Kids who are low in adaptability and high in emotional intensity, for example, are more likely to scream in anger when they don't get what they want than to go off in a pout. Keep in mind that temperament is not completely fixed. The feedback children get from parents and the situations they encounter in their lives can eventually modify how they react. With practice, for example, kids can gradually learn not to give up so fast when they're frustrated.

Activity level. Is your child quiet or rambunctious and restless? Restless kids easily become emotionally revved up, overexcited, and out of control. It may be harder to tell what a quiet child is feeling.

Regularity. Predictable children eat, sleep, and rest at roughly the same time each day. At the other extreme are kids who are very irregular. Their moods often change suddenly and unpredictably.

Approach/Withdrawal. Does your child react to new people and places with caution or curiosity? Kids at the cautious end may feel fearful and shy and be clingy.

Adaptability. How does your child handle change? If he doesn't adapt easily he may have a hard time with a new teacher or school routine, while a more adaptable child may just go along with the changes.

Sensory threshold. How sensitive is your child to loud noises, bright lights, scratchy fabrics, or crowded places? Is she easily bothered by them—or not?

Mood. Kids can look at the world in a positive or negative way. Does your child wake up happy or grouchy? Is he usually serious, sullen, cranky, or cheerful?

Intensity. Does your child howl with pain when she's hurt or keep so quiet that you don't know she's ill until she's running a fever? Highly intense kids react more strongly to situations than others, laugh louder and cry longer.

Distractibility. If your son wakes up in a bad mood, can he allow himself to laugh when you put your shirt on backwards, or does he continue to sulk?

Persistence and attention span. Some children can work more steadily than others when faced with obstacles. Those who can't feel frustrated more quickly. On the other hand, negative kids with high persistence may keep on whining, crying, or making a scene longer than others do. ❑

How Does Home Environment Influence A Child's Moods?

Families have a prevailing mood and temperament just as an individual does, and many aspects of daily life reflect it. Whether everyone is usually calm or rushed, whether a family spends a lot of time doing fun things together or doesn't, how family members express or don't express emotions, whether they talk noisily or quietly, whether parents dwell on problems or focus on the good things in life in their conversations—all combine to create a distinct emotional climate at home that has a profound effect on kids' moods.

The Bateson family, for example, is fairly strict about manners, behavior, and rules. The household routine is very predictable. Their kids are pretty self-contained and calm, and when they do get upset or angry, they don't express it with a lot of drama.

The exuberant Feins embrace a cheerful view of the world and encourage noisy discussions at the dinner table in which much disagreement is tolerated. The kids, Judy and Ryan, greet most days with enthusiasm and feel confident that if they create a highly emotional scene it won't be viewed as the end of the world.

Dinner in the Ross household is, sadly, full of nitpicking. The air is thick with tension and anger that are never discussed. Not surprisingly, six-year-old Amy and ten-year-old Sara Ross are often anxious. Will one of their parents explode? What will happen if mom or dad does?

Parents set the emotional tone

Parents often forget that while what we *say* about emotions is important, how we *act* influences a home's emotional atmosphere more and speaks louder and more enduringly to our kids. Every day they scrutinize how we behave and take their cues from what they see. What happens when mom and dad don't agree? Are we quick to jump on each other? Or do we try to talk things over later, after our tempers have cooled? When we're sad or angry, do we say so? Or do we try to pretend everything is fine?

Creating a good emotional climate is often a balancing act. Confiding our worries in detail makes kids anxious, but if we don't talk about our emotions and the inevitable conflicts in family life at all, kids blame themselves and get upset whenever there's tension in the air.

Of course children, with their individual temperaments, affect this emotional atmosphere, too. A temperamentally grumpy child added to the Fein house would probably affect everyone else's cheerful mood. Sometimes people in a family are all emotionally similar; in others, everyone gets along despite their differences, while in others, styles clash to such an extent that it seems a wonder the family survives.

When there's trouble at home . . .

Kids' emotions and moods are also a barometer of situations at home that shake their security. Evan, for example, has had nightmares ever since his sick grandma came to live with his family. Seven-year-old Peggy became grumpy when her dad, under pressure at work, began acting distant at breakfast. Change is stressful and scary to kids, and they generally react by becoming fearful, worried, angry, anxious, or upset either at home—or at school. When Angie's parents separated, for example, her math grades dropped. She couldn't concentrate on her times tables because she was too busy worrying about when she'd see her dad again. Children who have a very low tolerance for stress may react the most strongly of all.

Improve your home's atmosphere

It's always worth taking time to assess your home's emotional climate and think about what you'd like it to be. Often we can't change a difficult home situation. But we can create a better emotional atmosphere for our kids (see pages 82-84) by giving them extra support. A predictable daily routine gives them something to count on when problems arise. Family celebrations contribute to loving feelings and a child's sense of security. Encouraging kids to express emotions doesn't mean we have to permit slamming doors. ❑

What do kids appreciate about their home's atmosphere?

- "I like it when we do fun things together, like go to the beach or to visit my grandparents," says Corinne, 6.
- "Everyone in my family plays music, but we all play different instruments. So we all listen to each other," says Jack, 9.
- "I like it when my parents don't make me do everything with the family. If they're going out and I want to go over to my friend's house instead of going with them, it's usually okay," says Lydia, 13.

Are Some Kids Happier & More Cheerful?

Eight-year-old Mary is a delight, one of those happy children who jump out of bed most mornings with a grin that makes parents want to smile right back. Like one of those weighted toys that bounces upright no matter how hard it's punched down, she always seems to find her center. "Mary is the kind of girl who will do fine and probably be happy no matter where she is," was how her teacher summed up Mary on her final report card. Her basically cheerful temperament surrounds her like emotional armor.

Wouldn't we all like our kids to have the emotional resilience that Mary has? There are few sights as satisfying and reassuring to us as the joyful face of our child. While inborn temperament counts, luckily other factors also account for a child's happiness.

Feeling accepted for who you are

Ten-year-old Don is happy, too, even though he's different from Mary. He's picky about the food he eats and the clothes he wears and is slow to warm up to people and situations; every school year, he takes a month or so to adapt to a new teacher. Nature didn't supply him with Mary's emotional padding, but he has a family that understands and accepts him, and parents who make an effort to figure out what he needs to make him happy. Rather than blame him for having sensitive skin, they buy soft cotton shirts that don't irritate him, they alert the teacher in advance to his slow adjustment period, and they explain changes that are looming on the horizon long before they happen so that he has time to prepare himself. As a result, though he doesn't express his happy feelings as exuberantly as Mary, he's usually in a good mood, is content with his friends, enjoys school, and takes satisfaction in his growing collection of bones and arrowheads.

When children feel accepted by their parents the way Don does, they feel emotionally secure—and that's a big source of happiness for kids.

Letting go of bad feelings

One quality that cheerful children—and adults—share is their ability to feel what they feel and then let their feelings of disappointment or sadness go. My neighbor's thirteen-year-old son, Tom, who's very serious about his music, came home upset one day after scoring poorly on an important music test. But after moping in his room for thirty minutes or so, he was out shooting baskets by the garage with his brother, laughing. A less happy child might have let the poor grade haunt him, causing a bad mood to settle around him like a bad cold.

We can help our kids let go of their feelings more quickly by simply acknowledging how they feel.

How kids explain what's happening

Later, in the kitchen, Tom shared his thoughts about why he'd messed up with his dad. "I didn't study nearly enough," he said, recalling that he'd watched a movie on TV the night before the test. "Before the next test I'm going to start studying three days ahead instead of waiting until the last minute. Then I know I'll do better."

Tom, like many happy kids, could come up with an explanation for what happened and a plan that he thinks will guarantee future success. A happy child isn't one who's never angry or upset, but rather one who can see a way past unhappiness and obstacles and has faith in his ability to make changes. This is an ability parents can help kids develop (see pages 78-79).

The value of limits and family time

Many parents fall into what one psychologist calls the Happiness Trap. We can't bear for our kids *not* to be happy, so we acquiesce when they whine, "If you really wanted me to be happy, you'd buy me this video game," or we give in when they beg to go to the mall. But children who always get everything they want aren't necessarily happier. In fact, they often up the ante to find out just what our limits are, and end up relieved and happier when we sometimes say "no," lovingly, and stick to it.

We also forget that kids are happier when they feel they contribute something of importance to their family. One mom recalls a rainy Saturday when she, her husband, and her two boys cleaned the basement together. It was hard work and the boys complained, but the family ended up telling jokes and whistling crazy songs together. Afterward, the boys were proud and happy they'd helped. ❑

ASK THE EXPERTS

Psychologist Martin E. P. Seligman, author of *The Optimistic Child*, says optimists and pessimists think in different ways.

- **Pessimists use words like "always" and "never," as in "I always do badly on math tests."**
  Optimists use words like "this time" and "occasionally," as in "This time I didn't do well on the math test."
- **Pessimists rely on global explanations, as in "I stink at sports."**
  Optimists rely on specific explanations, as in "I'm not a fast runner, so soccer isn't my sport."
- **Pessimists blame themselves and others for who they are, as in "I'm a lousy friend."**
  Optimists examine their behavior, as in "I wasn't being a good friend when I made fun of Michelle."

What Makes Kids Grumpy, Irritable, & Angry?

In the upstairs hall, twelve-year-old Miranda is steaming. "Mom," she yells, "John will not get out of the bathroom and he knows I have to get ready for the play!"

On Saturdays Toby's dad has been teaching him how to play tennis, but the nine-year-old is still having a hard time getting the ball over the net. He tries and tries, then ends up kicking the net and getting mad at his dad.

Six-year-old Gina's grouchiness often materializes when she feels hungry. But if her mom lets her have a snack before dinner, Gina doesn't want to sit at the dinner table. Then her mom insists, and Gina grumps while everyone else eats.

Do these stories sound familiar? To most parents they probably do. Sometimes it seems as though our kids can get angry over just about anything. On a typical day we're liable to witness expressions of anger that range from mild irritation to murderous rage. It helps to think of these as distress signals of a small or big problem, a red light that something is wrong. It may be a brief, intense storm of bad temper that fades away once that problem is solved. At other times it may last and last.

Discomfort and temperament

Being tired or hungry is frequently a trigger for grumpiness and irritability in some kids, especially five-, six-, and seven-year-olds. Overstimulation and exaggerated expectations are reasons why the birthday child so often bursts into tears or gets angry at his or her party.

But for others, like Gina, the cause is a temperament that's a poor fit with their family. Gina's parents and two brothers are people who like to eat at exactly the same time each day. Gina isn't, and she gets irritated when members of her family insist she march to the beat of their drum. Other kids are especially bothered by scratchy clothes, bright lights, and minor cuts and bruises. For people who aren't upset by these kinds of disturbances, it appears as if these kids are simply exaggerating things or being too sensitive. They're not.

When kids encounter obstacles

We've all watched children get angry when inanimate objects don't do what they want them to. Toys that won't stack, Lego pieces that won't snap together, and general frustration with the physical world and their limited control over it often moves five- and six-year-olds to anger.

Older kids, like Toby, feel the same kind of frustration when they are trying to learn a new skill. Think of all the daily challenges that confront school-age kids—learning to read, hit a baseball, jump rope, write their name. Rarely can they master any of these skills immediately. Some kids can persevere longer than others before they become so frustrated they get angry. Frustration is also

AGE FACTOR

❖ Children learn very quickly that anger is one of the most problematic emotions to express. Researchers report that by third grade, children are much less likely to express their anger to peers or adults than they were two years earlier.

behind the anger kids with undiagnosed learning disabilities so often feel when they don't understand a lesson in class or can't figure out how to do their homework.

Being confronted by something they don't like—such as having to set the table or share a brownie with a sibling or not getting a toy they wanted—is yet another cause of kids' anger.

When other people make kids angry

Like Miranda, many children (and adults) become angry as well as hurt when they think they're being treated badly by someone else. It's hard for kids to accept that friends and siblings often don't behave the way they want them to, and conflicts inevitably arise. James, for example, was furious when his cousin wouldn't abide by the rules when playing Monopoly. Kids ages five to thirteen feel especially angry (and hurt) when they are slighted or left out or when friends break their promises.

However, cause and effect aren't always obvious where anger is concerned. A boy who rudely pushes his little sister after school may not be mad at her at all. Instead he may be angry that the coach didn't let him pitch in gym class.

What about parents?

As we all know, parents are often the cause of kids' anger. After all, we're the ones who make them do things they don't want to do, like take out the garbage. But sometimes it's because we *are* unfair, as Damien thought his mom was when she made him go to bed at the same time as his younger sister. Unjust punishments, arbitrary decisions, and unreasonable expectations are common reasons why our kids get so furious with us—and all derive from feeling powerless.

Preteens, intent on establishing their autonomy and individuality, often become angry with any and all authority figures—parents, teachers, or coaches—who constrain their freedom. They resent having to dress appropriately, come home on time, follow a schedule. And now that they are beginning to think about abstract concepts, they are also moved to anger by what they perceive as the injustices and unfairness of the world in which they live. ❑

What Are Kids Most Afraid Of—& Why?

Monsters in the closet, ghosts on the stairs, getting lost and never finding your way home, being chased by *Tyrannosaurus rex*—childhood fears like these stalked us when we were children, and stalk our kids now. What children fear most changes from country to country, but fears of animals (including dinosaurs, lions, bears, and sharks), strangers, and kidnapping are very prevalent in nearly every society. Fears of nuclear war and terrorism also haunt many of today's children as the media brings the world and all its problems ever closer to home.

Most of us are concerned when our kids whimper plaintively, "Mom, I'm scared." So it helps to know that fears are a normal part of every child's experience and that they develop in a fairly predictable pattern. Kids often cycle in and out of fearful periods, which sometimes coincide with a stressful time either at home or at school.

Children's fears change with age

Six-year-old Eric, like many kids his age, insists on a night light and needs the door open and the sound of music to go to bed because he's afraid of the dark and the unknown. Why? By the age of five, kids realize they are tiny creatures in a world of giants. It's no wonder that they fear getting lost, being abandoned by those on whom they depend, and imagine there are creatures in the closet that could gobble them up. They're just beginning to understand feelings are inside them, and that these aren't apparent to everyone.

The unpredictable holds terrors for kids, too. Loud sounds and sudden movements, for example, trigger the startle reflex, which in turn triggers fear. Kids who fear clowns may actually be upset because they can't be sure what a clown will do next.

Animal fears surface in nightmares of bears, spiders, big dogs, or other animals. Like many adults, I can still remember my childhood nightmare that recurred most often—of being chased by an enormous lion that had escaped from the zoo.

Children also worry about their own bodies—Nate was terrified of seeing his blood when he cut himself, afraid all his blood would run out—and about enduring pain. (In truth, some children do feel pain much more intensely than others.) The fear of pain is why so many kids fear going to the dentist or doctor and having injections. After all, a shot *does* hurt!

New experiences and awareness

Most kids' fears are more concrete by second or third grade, rooted in their real experiences at school and in sports. Fear of the unknown takes on new dimensions. Before the school concert, for example, Richard had stage fright, and when Laura competed for the girls' ice hockey team, she was intimidated by the new coach, who had a gruff, stern manner. Kids begin to have many fears about their social life: Will a best friend betray a secret? Will the school bully corner them in the hall?

Kids' growing reasoning abilities and awareness also affect their fears. They better understand time and realize death is permanent, so dying is scary. But instead of worrying about dinosaurs eating them up, they're afraid of burglars breaking into the house or being left alone. Seven-year-old Matthew asks his mom,"What if you're not at the bus stop today to pick me up?"

"Go to Mrs. Lynch's house next door."

"What if she's not there, either?"

"Then go to the neighbors across the street and wait there until I get home."

"What if they're not home?"

Every answer spawns a new question and raises the frightening prospect that maybe there isn't always a solution.

Preteens and performance

"I'm afraid I won't get a hit during the All Star game." "I'm afraid people are gossiping about me." "I know I'm going to fail the math test!" If you have a preteen, you've probably heard some version of these fears. Performance, both in school and with peers, is one of the biggest sources of fear for these now self-conscious kids. Like Sandy, many kids develop a fear of public speaking—the number one fear of most adults. They're terribly afraid of causing disappointment and of not living up to their parents' and their own expectations.

At the same time, fears for their bodily safety diminish, at least on the surface. In fact, many kids harbor a fear of being permanently hurt, such as paralyzed for life.

Childhood fears are changing

Most of us are highly aware how events on the nightly news inspire fear in our kids and cause nightmares. Across the country, children of all ages were traumatized by the bombing of the Oklahoma City federal building and the explosion that destroyed TWA flight 800 over the ocean in 1996. Events like these give children's amorphous fears of destruction and death very concrete form. In fact, when psychologist Patricia Owen recently surveyed third and fourth graders from low-income and middle-class neighborhoods to discover their biggest fears, she was surprised to find they listed fears typical of older kids: they were afraid of drugs, gangs, drive-by shootings, gunshots, and nuclear weapons.

The uses of fear

Too much fear in kids is paralyzing—but too little can be dangerous. Though it isn't a pleasant emotion, some fear is essential for our kids' survival. After all, fear is what makes us look before we cross the street. There are situations in which we *don't* want our kids to lose their fears. ❑

DID YOU KNOW?

- Psychologist Patricia Owen of St. Mary's University in San Antonio, Texas, has studied children's fears in Bali, Burma, Cambodia, Laos, Mexico, Mongolia, and San Antonio, Texas. In all these places she found girls consistently list more fears than boys do and that they rate their fears as more intense than boys.
- Research indicates that 38% of children become markedly more fearful in the year after the birth of a sibling.
- The American Psychological Association estimates that the average child has seen 8,000 murders and over 100,000 other violent acts on TV by the time he or she is 12 years old.

What Do Kids Worry About?

Michelle's parents joke that she was born with a frown on her face. Her brothers call her a "worry wart" because she worries about so many different things, and once she starts she can't seem to stop! When all the kids in the fifth grade had to memorize a short quote to recite at an assembly, Michelle was anxious for two weeks. Maybe she would get laryngitis. Maybe she would forget the words. Maybe she would trip as she walked out on the stage. What, her parents wondered, was really worrying her?

Kids' worries are more shapeless than their fears. Children can usually name very specifically the things they're afraid of—spiders, the dark, nightmares, nuclear war. What our kids are anxious about is harder to put a finger on because often kids themselves don't know and they talk about it in vague terms.

A way of thinking

Some children—about ten percent—*are* temperamentally more anxious than others, the way Michelle is. Unusually sensitive to any sign of danger, they show extreme caution in a new situation and react to new people as though they were a threat, even if there is no reason to. But all kids who worry share a way of thinking and talking about the world. Like Michelle, they rehearse what could go wrong in a situation and expect it to happen. When they anticipate "What if . . .?" they fill in the blank with the worst-case scenario. For many the trigger for this kind of anxiety is a stressful event in the near future, such as starting kindergarten or moving.

Common themes

Often a child's anxieties have a common theme. For a few months five-year-old Jay's centered on his body. If he skinned his knee or cut himself, he worried that he might bleed too much. When he had a stomachache, he kept asking his mom, "What if I throw up?" Concerns about losing control of their bodies are very normal in young children.

Not surprisingly, being rejected by friends or supplanted in the family, particularly when there's a new baby in the house or a parent remarries and another child moves in, is another source of anxiety. Young children also worry about their own power to make things happen. Lewis, for example, was worried when his mom and dad had a big argument because he was sure he'd caused it.

Social anxieties

About ten to twenty percent of kids are born temperamentally shy. Highly self-conscious, they worry most about situations where they might be embarrassed or judged. But by mid-elementary school, *all* children are very concerned about

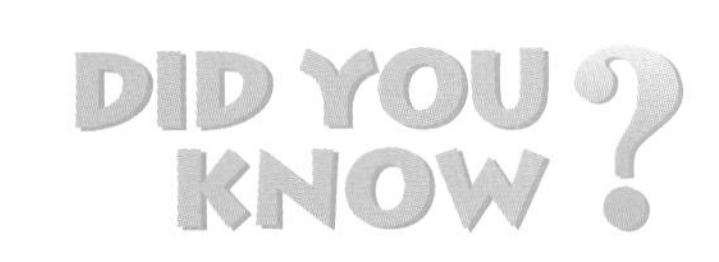

Caffeine is the only food substance that has been shown consistently to increase anxiety. It causes a rapid heartbeat, rapid breathing, dizziness, and other physical reactions associated with anxiety.

their social standing, and their worries center on whether they will be accepted. Jill, like many kids, was highly attuned to who's "in" and who's "out" by the time she entered fourth grade. No wonder preteens spend so many jittery hours worrying that they won't be invited to an important party or that they'll buy the wrong kind of jeans.

Performance anxiety

Second to social apprehension are kids' worries about how well they'll perform at school, on the basketball court, on stage. Will they look stupid? That was Michelle's real concern. As schoolwork pressures increase, so does anxiety—about tests, about math, about making the honor roll. "Fourth grade is so much harder," moaned my son. Even though he brought home generally good grades, he still worried about how he'd do on the next report card.

Paradoxically, children also feel anxious when good things happen to them. When Tony earned the sportsmanship award for a good soccer season, he said to his dad, "Gee, I did okay this time, but what happens if I disappoint everyone next year?"

Family worries

By the time children turn eleven, it's almost impossible to keep parental anxieties from seeping into their awareness. When Elizabeth's dad was worried about his job because his company was downsizing, she worried, too, imagining they would have to sell their house and she'd have to leave her friends. And even preteens from the most stable homes worry when they overhear parents fighting. Will they get a divorce as so many of their friends' parents have?

Global concerns

Today, our children are also highly aware of threats to our world in the form of pollution, terrorism, endangered species, and the disappearance of the rain forest—and these worry them, too. ❑

- "I worry about a lot of things. I worry that I'll mess up a drawing I'm working on, or that the computer will break, that someone will beat me up, or dare me to do something I don't want to do," explains Jonathan, 8.
- "I worry that people won't believe me even when I'm telling the truth," says Margaret, 13.

What's The Difference Between Being Sad & Being Depressed?

Sadness is our children's knee-jerk reaction to loss, just as it is for adults. That's why six-year-old Marie felt so unhappy after she left her favorite teddy bear in a busy airport and it didn't turn up in the lost-and-found. Roger, an eleven-year-old science whiz, was unhappy because he expected to win the prize at the school science fair, and didn't. At first he was mad at the judges, but then disappointment took over, and he sadly told his mom, "Maybe I won't be a scientist when I grow up."

Our kids often hibernate emotionally when they're sad by curling up, slowing down, and licking their wounds. Anger, happiness, jealousy, and fear move them to outward expression. But in the midst of loss our children don't feel like doing much of anything, because there's nothing much to do. They know they can't recover the lost bear or get the prize. They feel powerless, ache inside, and turn inward.

The hard part for parents is letting our kids feel that way. But we can't shield them from sadness nor can we make it go away.

Sadness is a part of childhood

Every child has times when he or she feels blue and down in the dumps. Failure, disappointment, and death occur in our kids' lives, just as they do in ours. Pets run away, birthday parties end, favorite

toys break, your child doesn't get elected president of the class after campaigning for three weeks or get the starring role in the musical at camp or make the A hockey team or get invited to the eighth-grade dance by the boy she favors. Not only that—parents fight and divorce, a favorite aunt becomes ill and dies.

Sometimes sadness shows up in our kids at surprising times. Moments before Max's sixth birthday party, he burst into tears as the first guest pulled in the driveway. He couldn't explain why he was crying, and his dad put it down to overexcitement. But when the party was over, Max said he'd waited so long for the party, and he knew it would be over so soon, and he didn't want it to. Even five-year-olds can anticipate loss and feel its sting.

Events that seem minor to us can make children unhappy, too. Nine-year-old Marcie, for example, was crushed when she learned that her best friend, Jo, was moving to a new house in the same neighborhood. "It's not so bad. You'll still be at the same school," Marcie's mom pointed out. But Marcie wasn't consoled. "It just won't be the same," she said sadly.

The many faces of sadness

All parents recognize the many telltale sad signs in our kids—the hot tears, the glum face, the quivering lips, the slumped, defeated posture of the shoulders, the shut door to a child's room and music wafting out from the CD player. But even if children don't act sad that doesn't mean they're not feeling blue. In fact, many kids between the ages of five and thirteen who pick fights or continually complain of aches and pains really feel sad inside.

Or maybe they're like eight-year-old Sam, who seemed impassive when his beloved dog, Boomer, died. Boomer had been a part of the family since Sam was a baby, and Sam even used to drink his bottle using the dog as a pillow. Sam's parents were worried that Sam would fall apart. To their surprise, Sam simply said, "I knew he would die sometime," and proceeded to play with his action figures.

Like many kids, Sam felt overwhelmed and needed time to sift through his emotions before he could allow himself to miss Boomer and feel sad. Sure enough, about a month later, he got into a fight with his dad over keeping his big overhead light on all night, and explained as he started to cry, "I need to keep the light on so Boomer can find his way home."

Who kids tell—and why

Until about age eight, both boys and girls are equally likely to let sadness show on their faces. But when boys turn nine or ten, they usually start keeping their sad feelings to themselves, as they do most other feelings except for anger. However,

ASK THE EXPERTS

Denver psychologist Susan Heitler, author of *Depression, A Disorder of Power,* says:

- **In some people depression emerges because of a genetic predisposition. Particularly in these cases, medications such as Prozac have proven very effective.**
- **Many cases of depression in kids are triggered by a feeling of powerlessness in a difficult situation.**
- **If a child appears depressed, parents can help by encouraging him or her to identify the situation that's triggering feelings of powerlessness. Then, together, they can brainstorm actions each can take to address the problem.**

if kids feel very close to their parents, they're likely to discuss their sad feelings with them until they're about eleven. (If they're only close to one parent, they tend to confide in that parent.)

As they enter adolescence, kids close up. Boys especially tend not to talk at all, and instead they often seek comfort in just hanging out with their dads. Girls, who are more comfortable articulating their feelings, tend to reveal sadness to their moms.

When sadness lingers

As most parents discover, the best remedy for sadness is love, understanding, and the passage of time. Most kids recover from a disappointment or failure in a few days, but sadness over losses such as a grandparent's death or their parents' divorce lasts a long time. Even after a child seems to have accepted it, one small event can trigger a return of these feelings. If a sad mood takes hold, parents can help by being patient and available. But if the mood prevents your child from engaging in his or her usual activities—an honor roll student stops studying or a soccer player starts missing practice—seek help.

Depression is more complex

Depression isn't simply lingering sadness, even if it often begins that way. Other feelings compound it—anger, frustration, resentment, and perhaps most significantly, powerlessness. Most psychologists agree that depression is caused by many different factors, including stressful events, genetics, a negative way of thinking, and experiences that lead kids to believe that they can't influence events in their lives. In time, they start thinking and talking about themselves in negative terms: "I'm nothing." "I always do everything wrong." "No one likes me." "Nothing I do matters."

Signs your child is depressed

Children rarely announce, "I'm depressed." Instead they reveal their unhappiness through sometimes dramatic changes in moods, words, and behavior that last for several weeks or more.

One of the most immediate symptoms parents notice is withdrawal. Mary Sue's experience with her twelve-year-old daughter, Lark, was typical. "I suddenly realized that instead of coming home from school and calling a friend, Lark was retreating to her room to watch TV," Mary Sue recalls. When friends phoned, Lark spoke for a minute or two, hanging up without any prompting from her mom or dad. If Mary Sue suggested shopping or a movie, Lark declined. To her mom, it looked as if her daughter was losing her zest for life.

Most kids who are depressed don't necessarily act depressed every minute of the day. They may enjoy playing a basketball game, for example, but they

DID YOU KNOW?

- Two University of Pittsburgh psychologists found in their studies that people diagnosed with depression had one "bad" thought for every "good" thought. People who weren't depressed, on the other hand, had twice as many good thoughts as bad ones.
- A recent study found that 9% of 12- to 14-year-olds suffer from full-blown depressive disorders.

tend to react in the same flat way to most things, whether a party, a present, a try-out for a team, or a bad report card. Over time adolescents may begin expressing pessimism about their future, with comments like "I guess I'll never make it to college" or even "What's the point of trying? There's nothing to live for."

Physical symptoms are a clue

Not all signs of depression are so easy to detect. Often, children may seem as if they're simply sad or tired. But if their lethargy lingers beyond what you feel is natural, then take a look at your child's physical habits and complaints. Five-year-old Liza, who'd been toilet trained at night for two years, suddenly began wetting her bed again. Seven-year-old Marcus began complaining of headaches and stomachaches. Ten-year-old David couldn't get to sleep and when he finally did, frequently had bad dreams. Thirteen-year-old Olivia lost her appetite. No matter what was served, she picked at her food.

What about behavior?

Irritability, sudden outbursts of temper, general restlessness, and even overactivity are signs of depression in younger children. Preteens who have been doing well usually stop doing what they've been doing. Lark, for example, had been a good student, but her grades plummeted. She didn't study for tests and neglected her homework. Kevin, a basketball player, left the team and avoided the teammates he'd been close to. Others drop out of activities they used to enjoy or get into fights.

Of course, listlessness that lasts a week or so, occasional despairing comments, or a few days with no appetite doesn't necessarily mean that your child is depressed. After all, kids on the cusp of adolescence *are* moody. And if your child is doing well everywhere but home, he or she is probably okay. But if symptoms last for three to four weeks without letting up and interfere with your child's life at school and with friends as well as at home, then they may be signs that your child is depressed.

Consult your doctor

Lark's mom followed the steps that experts recommend when parents suspect their child is depressed. She first made an appointment with Lark's pediatrician. Many symptoms of depression are actually caused by an undiagnosed illness or allergy, a learning disability, or attention deficit disorder rather than psychological problems.

Once physical causes are ruled out, ask your doctor to refer you to a psychologist who specializes in working with children. Or ask the psychologist at your child's school—all schools have one—to see your child, and if necessary make a referral to a private practitioner or a clinic. ❑

- "I get sad when my friend or my sister is sick, and I can't play with them," reports Katie, 7.
- "I'm sad when my brother hits me or says mean things to me. What he says makes me sadder than what he does," says Matt, 9.
- "I'm sad after I read books about people dying or being kidnapped, or about the Holocaust," says Lucy, 12.

Why Are Kids In Middle School So Moody?

Sometimes, it seems as if our kids become moody adolescents overnight. Suddenly the bedroom door is closed, the phone is always in use, and every question you pose has a one-word answer—"Fine"—delivered with plenty of attitude.

This huge transition coincides with the years of middle or junior high school. Children begin to recognize they're leaving their childhood behind—their bodies are changing outwardly and hormonally as well. And they're beginning the long, sometimes painful, process of separating from their parents.

If you look back to your own childhood, you may remember how hard this time of self-definition is. Everything is in a state of flux, including how our kids think and feel from moment to moment.

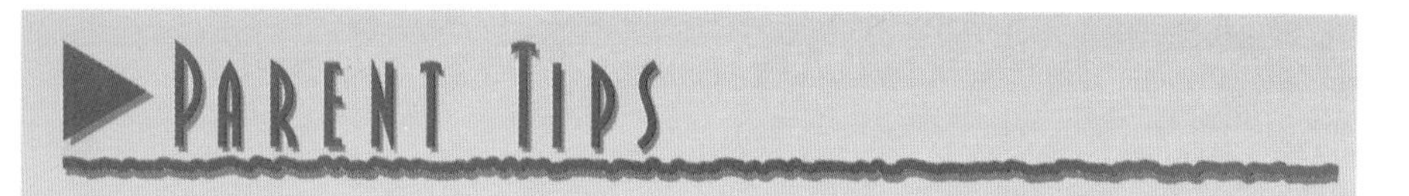

How some parents cope with moody kids:

- "I try to remember how miserable I was in 7th grade," says Don, father of 2 boys and a girl.
- "I lay down some very basic ground rules: you have to be polite, you have to clean up after yourself," reports Martha, mother of 2 girls.
- "I remind myself that not every battle is worth fighting," says John, father of a boy and a girl.
- "I tell myself that the more attached a child feels, the harder it is to break away," offers Melinda, mother of a boy.

Mood swings are common

As parents soon realize, one reason kids' moods shift so often is that our children go back and forth between wanting to be "grown up" and independent and retreating back to childhood for reassurance, as twelve-year-old Brian did. One night when his mom came into his room, as usual, to say good night, he snarled, "I'm not a baby any more. Just say goodnight from there."

Elaine, stunned and hurt, did exactly that for the next week or so. But on Sunday night, her son called out, "Mommy want to come give Brian a kiss goodnight?" just as if he were three years old again.

"I've come to accept the fact that I never know which child will be in bed at night," Elaine concludes, "or come down to breakfast, or home from school."

In truth, Brian doesn't know who he is, either. Adolescence is the time when kids try on the trappings of many different people, trying to find the right fit—and moodiness is part of this process.

Self-consciousness affects moods

One parent describes adolescence as the "terrible twos" revisited. That's fairly accurate. A two-year-old is learning his place in the world, as well as the limits of his capabilities. Our kids in middle school are making the same discovery, unfortunately with the added factor of self-consciousness. When two-year-olds—or even ten-year-olds—

feel sad, they're not always aware of their feelings—they cry, feel listless, or complain of a tummyache. But middle schoolers are painfully aware of how sad they feel. They're also aware of how much their feelings have an impact on others—friends, family, teachers—and how much other people's feelings have an impact on them.

Their self-consciousness extends to how their own physical maturity and size compare to those of other kids. No one wants to be "weird." Sheila, a seventh grader, is in despair that she still hasn't gotten her period the way her friend Joan has. George worries about how soon he'll be taller than the girls in his class.

Day-to-day life for many kids feels as if they live in an echo chamber where every spoken word and gesture reverberates endlessly. Everything they say and do—and feel—is held up for scrutiny and judgment, especially by themselves. No wonder kids react by being so moody!

New social pressures

Until middle school, children care mostly about their parents' judgments and opinions. But one of the hallmarks of adolescence is the fact that children who were previously very independent thinkers suddenly become slaves to the peer group. Being "accepted" is their only goal. They're now looking for friends like themselves, and a friend often turns out to be different than they thought, so allegiances change quickly. Researchers think girls may be especially vulnerable to the agonies of rejection. If our kids aren't "in" with the right group this week, you can bet their bad moods will be turned on full blast at home for us.

To most parents, like Brian's mom, Elaine, it often feels as if the full brunt of their preteens' moodiness is directed at them. But teens are moody toward each other, too.

Rigid thinking

Children in middle school tend to be absolutists, seeing everything in black-and-white terms. Thirteen-year-old Lily isn't much interested in shades of meaning—her hair is either "perfect" or a "disaster," her parents are either "great" or "total phonies." Being labeled a phony is one of the worst accusations teens can make about each other or their parents and teachers. This kind of rigid thinking leaves kids very vulnerable to moodiness.

New ways to connect

Though all kids in this age group want to feel independent from their parents, they also want new ways to feel attached. Since they don't know how to achieve this, they swing from being loving to accusing in a flash. The challenge for us as parents is to find inventive ways to be close without being intrusive. ❑

What makes you moody?

- "I hate it when my parents like what I do—my songs, my clothes, TV shows," says Jeff, 13.
- "When my mom keeps using all this psychological language with me, asking, 'How do you feel about that?'" says Jane, 12.
- "When my best friend acts like a traitor and hangs out with somebody else," reports Denise, 11.

Do Moods Affect Kids' Schoolwork, Friendships, & Health?

Most parents probably won't be surprised to hear that children who can control their emotions and know how to respond to other kids' feelings have more friends. But did you know they also do better academically and even have better overall health? That's why it's important to help our kids understand the ways their emotions affect the important parts of their lives.

In the classroom

Kids spend most of the day in school, and how they feel when they are there has a profound effect on what they learn. Lee, who is easily frustrated and wants to quit working when confronted with a tough problem, has a harder time with schoolwork and routines than Bill, who faces learning new subjects and skills with confidence and a positive outlook. Of course, few of our children feel the way Bill does all the time!

When children are depressed, worried, or angry about something that's going on in their lives, or are afraid of a teacher, their emotions take up most of their mental energy. As a result, they may have difficulty paying attention in class, memorizing, and absorbing facts. Children who are anxious about performing and who can't calm themselves down sometimes panic when they have to read aloud or give an oral report and often do poorly on tests. The result is usually bad grades. Students who can't control their anger may act up in class by talking back to a teacher or lashing out at another student and become discipline problems.

Because both trouble at home and at school influence kids' moods and emotions, both also have an impact on what kids learn and how they behave in the classroom. A child who's afraid the school bully will pick on him in the hall right after social studies probably won't remember much from that class. Mark, a fourth grader, has stopped trying to do his best because he is so angry at the way his grumpy teacher "chews me out over nothing." Kids who repeatedly come home angry and depressed, saying "I'll never learn to read," may have learning disabilities the teacher hasn't recognized.

Sometimes we forget how frequently our kids bring their worries about problems at home with them to school. When Emily's parents separated and her dad moved to an apartment, Emily was so concerned about how often she'd see him that she often forgot to write down homework assignments and spent math class daydreaming.

Friendships

Every girl in the third grade wants to be Jennifer's friend. No wonder! She's fun to be with because she's usually happy and outgoing, and when you have an argument with her, she gets over it fast and apologizes. Psychologists have found that boys and girls like Jennifer, who know how to manage their feelings and have a positive outlook, are the best liked in any class. Kids, in other words, are drawn to children who are emotionally competent.

Four kinds of kids have trouble making and keeping friends—and all have problems with moods and emotions.

Bob, a fifth grader, becomes aggressive whenever he becomes embroiled in a conflict, and once he even kicked a classmate in the ribs. Kids like Bob, who have trouble managing their anger, are the most likely to be rejected by other kids and are usually disliked by teachers.

Shy and timid children, on the other hand, are mostly ignored. Norma, for example, lurks around the edges of activities on the playground at recess because she's afraid to approach other kids.

Anxious children, like eleven-year-old Alan, give off an air of vulnerability that bullies often zero in on.

Lou Anne's friends have stopped calling her. Like most kids who suffer from depression, Lou Anne has withdrawn from them and doesn't return their phone calls. Besides, her sadness makes her friends feel so sad they don't want to be around her. As a result she's missing out on the social activity that's so important to preteens.

Stress and health

We've all become aware in recent years of the connections between stress and physical health. So it's worth remembering that children who feel at the mercy of their moods usually end up feeling more stressed-out than those who have learned to calm themselves down and find other ways to handle their emotions. Alan, who's usually anxious about something, is plagued by headaches and stomachaches, for example. Stress also affects the immune system, making our kids (and us) more susceptible to many contagious illnesses, such as colds, flu, and infections.

The power of positive emotions

Using their emotions in good ways helps kids succeed in school and with friends, and improves health, and this can affect their lives far beyond elementary and middle school. During those early years their patterns of learning and reacting to people and situations are set in motion. Some children *do* have a harder time managing their emotions than others, but if parents help kids understand their emotions, they can learn to use them in positive, rather than negative, ways (see pages 48-79). ❑

DID YOU KNOW?

◆ Dr. Jacqueline Bartlett, an associate professor of psychiatry at New Jersey Medical School, researched the effects of stress on children's immune systems in 1997 by studying granulocytes, the cells that fight bacterial infections. In a group of 36 children, those whose parents had divorced or separated had granulocytes that were less able to kill bacteria than children who were under less stress.

Do Moody Kids Grow Up To Be Moody Adults?

We all know people who haven't really changed much throughout the years. My sister, an attorney and mother of two, has some of the traits she had at seven—she's still slow to get angry, intensely competitive, somewhat moody, with a mildly pessimistic view of life.

But she's also changed in many essential ways. She no longer always expects the worst to happen, for example, and her grumpy moods aren't nearly as frequent.

Though temperament and basic mood are part of our kids' genetic makeup, children don't have to be slaves to biology. Like my sister, a "moody" child isn't necessarily doomed to be a moody adult.

What makes the difference?

With coaching, support, safe experiences, and gradual steps toward change, most kids can develop the skills they need to tame a hot temper, tone down grumpiness, or soothe anxiety. But this won't completely eradicate a child's basic nature.

Rosemary's parents, for example, taught her ways to overcome some of her social anxiety. As a ten-year-old, she hated large gatherings. The prospect of meeting many new people made her freeze up with fear. Instead of expecting her to make conversation with everyone at their parties, her parents gave her a job to do. All she had to say to each guest was, "May I have your coat?" and then take it into the bedroom.

Rosemary felt proud of her role; she knew her parents were depending on her. At the same time, because she wasn't worried about having to make conversation with strangers, she relaxed just enough to notice that the adults smiled at her and said kind things. Though she wasn't entirely comfortable, she could handle the situation.

Gradually, with experience, she realized that facing a room of strangers wasn't as terrifying as she'd once thought. She could quell her anxiety by assigning herself a specific role. Each time she gained a little more confidence and by the time she left home for college, no one would have described her as someone who was afraid of strangers, even though she hadn't turned into an exuberant, outgoing person.

For others, experiences away from home, such as spending summers at a camp with friendly counselors, encourage them to try new ways of reacting.

When moods persists

Without help, some kids change very little. About two percent of shy, sensitive kids develop anxiety disorders. Kids who are lonely, anxious, or depressed may carry feelings of low self-esteem into adulthood. In a long-term study of 870 boys, psychologist Leonard Eron and others found that boys who were hostile toward others at the age of eight were more likely to be in trouble with the law fifteen years later. ❑

DID YOU KNOW?

◆ According to Dr. Jerome Kagan, a developmental psychologist at Harvard University, there is "only a small, modest relationship between an infant's temperament in the first year of life and his or her emotional style when older. In other words, if your baby was extra sensitive and difficult during his first year of life, that doesn't necessarily mean he'll be that way forever."

WHAT TO DO

The Best Advice

Clues To Your Child's Feelings

For parents, each child's moods and emotions are a book they have to learn how to read. In the beginning, the book seems remarkably easy. "You look pretty angry," I said to my son once when he came steaming downstairs after a terrible—and loud—fight with his older brother.

"How do you know?" he growled at me, genuinely surprised. At three he had no clue that he had "angry" written all over his face. Before the age of five, most kids are as unself-conscious and direct about how they're feeling as my son was; we can often tell at a glance whether they're happy or jealous, sad or disappointed by the expression on a face or the set of their shoulders. And they're often quick to let us know how bad or good they feel, even if they can't tell us why. Some kids continue to wear their hearts on their sleeves as they grow, but many don't. With each passing year our task usually becomes a little harder—the facial expressions more difficult to interpret, the other clues to their feelings more subtle.

When kids are hard to read

As they get older, kids learn *not* to express everything they're feeling. In fact, they discover that in certain situations they'd better cover up what they feel! Six-year-old Valerie doesn't wrinkle her nose at a treat she doesn't like at a friend's birthday party. Instead, she takes it and says "Thank you," because she knows that this is polite.

Sometimes children express their feelings indirectly. For example, to be accepted by the boys in his class, eight-year-old Tony knew he had to keep his "cool" and not show how angry being teased made him feel. So he began taking his anger out on his sister by teasing *her*. This was puzzling to his parents—until they discovered that Tony was being teased at school.

Kids may be too embarrassed to share what's really worrying them, like the fight their parents had last night. And sometimes they don't know what they're feeling.

When a child is hard to read, parents have to become detectives, alert to all sorts of physical and behavioral clues to their feelings. Is your child eating well? Sleeping

Parent Tips

- "I spend 10 minutes each evening comparing notes with my husband—who seemed cranky, who might be getting sick, who had a fight with a friend. That way, we can track problems early," says Ann, mother of 3.
- "I ask my daughter to select a CD to listen to while we clean up after dinner. The type of music she selects—upbeat, slow—is a pretty accurate key to her mood that day," explains Tanya, mother of a daughter.
- "I bought diaries for my kids, and they get to stay up an extra 10 minutes past their bedtime to write in them. After they're done, they usually feel like talking to me about what they wrote," says Don, father of 2.

well? Snapping at her brother for no reason? Complaining about headaches? Struggling with homework? In trouble at school? For five-, six-, and seven-year-olds, their fantasy play is often a window onto how and what they are feeling.

Getting kids to open up

Talking about strong emotions isn't easy for kids, but choosing the right moment can help. In our house that means when my sons seem relaxed and I have time to really listen. Many young children let their guard down while taking a bath or just before sleep. Other good times are while cleaning up together after dinner, driving to sports practice, or hiking.

Asking the right questions is important. If they're too general, as in "How are you feeling?" you may hear the requisite "Fine," and the conversation will be over before it started. Experts suggest asking about events first, using specific questions: "How was that spelling test you had today?" or "Did that kid who bothered you on the bus yesterday say anything to you today?" Chances are that as your child retells what happened, he or she will be more ready to answer "How did that make you feel?"

Comments like "I thought your friend Alan seemed touchy today. How did he seem to you?" on a day when your child had trouble with a friend may lead from a discussion of Alan's mood to your son's.

What about reticent preteens?

Until about age eleven, most children are pretty forthcoming if asked the right questions. But with the onset of puberty comes a strange silence. Suddenly questions such as "What's wrong?" are perceived as highly intrusive. That's when we need to become extra creative about getting information.

One essential tactic is to make sure that there's a time every day when your kids know you're available. Another is to begin talking about an impersonal subject, such as something on a TV show that evokes a strong emotion. Discussing a movie or a song that got your own emotions going works, too. A friend of mine often tries relating a story from his own day—as in "Boy, my boss made me so furious today!"—and usually finds his preteen daughter will chime in with a story of her own.

Know your child

There's no shortcut to understanding our kids' emotions and moods. To ask the kinds of questions that get them to open up you have to know how they usually react to events and be on top of the little details of their lives—who their best buddies are this week, whether they're finding the times tables frustrating to learn, which teachers they like and which are a pain, what situations usually worry them. Then when they can't say what's bothering them, you have a place to start. ❑

- "Sometimes when I'm feeling angry, I get really quiet. It's like I can't talk. I just nod 'yes' and 'no' when my parents ask me questions," says Nancy, 8.
- "When I'm upset, I don't say anything. I go into my room and get in my bed and under the covers," says Beth, 11.
- "When I'm worried about a test coming up in school, I lose my appetite," says Mark, 13.

Be An "Emotion Coach"

All kids in elementary and middle school have difficulty with their moods and emotions—at least part of the time—at school, at home, and with friends. Sometimes kids, even those who are usually sensitive, have trouble identifying what they're feeling and why. And sometimes they have trouble managing their feelings, the way twelve-year-old Emily did one day in science. She became so upset at her lab partner that she tore up the paper with their findings. As a result they received a zero for the lab, and Emily lost a friend.

Most parents want their children to understand their feelings and learn to express them without alienating others. But many of us don't realize that how we listen, respond, and guide them when their emotions run hot is the way they learn the most. Washington State psychologist Dr. John Gottman, who has extensively researched ways parents can effectively help their children increase their emotional intelligence, calls this "emotion coaching."

Use emotional moments

First we have to be willing to acknowledge when our kids *are* angry, upset, afraid, or feeling blue. For example, though it may be tempting to minimize your son's disappointment when a friend can't come over by saying, "You can play another day," Gottman suggests parents think of such small events as opportunities to teach kids important lessons in handling their feelings. But pick the time well. When we're tired, rushed, or upset ourselves, we can't pay enough attention to our kids to do a very good coaching job!

Catching emotions at a low intensity level, as Margaret did, is the best way. She realized her ten-year-old son, Bobby, was becoming increasingly nervous about leaving for Boy Scout camp even though the departure date was a week away. Rather than wait for a scene at the bus, she casually brought up the topic of camp several times during the week, so Bobby could talk about feeling nervous if he wanted to.

Listen with empathy

Part of being an emotion coach is learning when to do nothing but listen. Our kids are at their most vulnerable when they're emotional, whether sad or angry, happy or jealous, just as adults are. Often all they really want is for someone—especially mom or dad—to listen and say, "I hear you. I understand what you're saying. Sometimes I feel that way, too."

Being accepting of the way your child sees things and trying to understand a situation from his or her point of view is a key part of listening when kids' emotions run high. And that means letting them express how they feel without judging, criticizing, contradicting, or trying to fix the problem—something some of us, like Alissa's mom, find hard to do.

Alissa's younger sister, Ilene, has been picking up the extension phone and listening in on Alissa's conversations with a boy in her class. Ilene finally announced her presence with a giggle, and when Alissa got off the phone, she was shaking with anger. "I hate her!" she raged to her mother. "I never want to see Ilene again!"

"You don't mean that," her mother argued. "You know you love your sister." It was a logical answer, but it didn't express much understanding of what Alissa was feeling at that moment.

Suppose her mom had simply said, "I'd be furious, too. Listening in on private conversations is wrong no matter who does it. We'll talk about what to do about this later." Chances are, say researchers, that Alissa would have immediately felt calmer because she could trust her mom to understand how she feels.

Help kids label how they feel

Researchers have discovered that just naming the emotion a child is feeling has a soothing effect on his nervous system and even helps him recover his equilibrium more quickly. This is especially true for children between the ages of five and eleven. Six-year-old Michael, for example, has a new baby brother. He doesn't know that the defiant, slightly angry, slightly sad feeling he has is jealousy—he just squeezes himself onto his mother's lap while she's nursing the infant. It's only when his mom says affectionately, "I think

ASK THE EXPERTS

In his study of 56 families, Dr. John Gottman found that children of parents who acted as "emotion coaches":

- **scored higher in math and reading**
- **had better social skills**
- **got along better with friends**
- **had lower levels of stress-related hormones in their urine**
- **were less likely to have colds and flu.**

DID YOU KNOW?

How dads affect kids' emotions:

- Many psychologists believe that the roughhousing fathers do with their kids helps children learn about emotions.
- Kids whose dads are warm and involved are likely to have better social relationships throughout their lives.
- When fathers are cold and mocking, their kids are more likely to get into trouble at school and behave aggressively toward friends.

you're feeling a little jealous of the baby," that he realizes his feeling has a name. Being able to translate vague feelings into something definable gives kids a sense of mastery—they feel less at the mercy of how they feel and more in control.

This is true for mixed emotions, too. Few of us actually feel only one feeling at a time. A child about to enter middle school is proud of all she's achieved but also nervous of what's ahead. Kids don't necessarily understand that two feelings don't cancel each other out but can exist side by side. Even older kids are reassured when we remind them it's normal to be annoyed and angry at a friend but still like him or her.

Set limits on behavior

While it's not wrong to feel a certain way, most parents don't want kids to act on their feelings in hurtful ways. Accepting the feelings, however, doesn't mean we accept their behavior as appropriate. That's why another essential in emotion coaching is letting our kids know what's not allowed, like destroying someone's paper the way Emily did in her science lab or making cutting and hurtful remarks. Every family has its own list of absolute noes. One good technique is to remind kids of the consequences of rash behavior, as Fred did. He told his son, "When you lose your temper and throw a book across the room, you run the risk of ruining the book and breaking something in the living room." Of course, for some behaviors parents have to set the consequences, as in "Hitting means a fifteen-minute time-out!"

Try problem solving

The other side of setting limits is helping kids figure out what they *can* do. Instead of yelling at you, perhaps your daughter could post a list of her grievances about you on the refrigerator. No matter what the emotion, it pays to help your child decide what he or she wants to accomplish. Alissa, for example, thought she wanted revenge, but her real goal was to keep her sister from listening in on her private calls.

Brainstorm solutions, and then decide which course of action is best. Though parents are usually tempted to jump in with a solution, research has shown that kids are more likely to change the way they act if they come up with an idea themselves.

Don't forget the power of humor! Social psychologist Carol Tavris describes how her father helped her gain a lighter perspective on her emotions by taking her to a Charlie Chaplin movie. Laughing out loud dissipated her sullen mood.

Make time for play

It's true that kids' moods can simply pass on their own. Until the age of eight or nine, kids often use play to resolve anxiety, anger, and other feelings. Think of how they sometimes work through their anger at us by scolding their stuffed animals! But today kids' lives are often so filled with scheduled activities that they don't have enough unstructured time for this kind of play. Part of emotion coaching is making sure they do—and joining in when they want us to. Even older kids need "down" time to sort through their emotions.

What not to do

The night of my son's induction to the Junior Honor Society he was standing at the reception with his best friend, Ted, and both looked very proud of themselves. Then Ted's dad said, "So, they let you two into the honor society. What were the qualifications? You had to sign your names?"

My son knew it was a joke—and so did Ted, sort of. But I saw the hurt in Ted's eyes. On his night of triumph, he wanted praise from his father, not sarcasm.

Parents sometimes forget how much children take even the mildest sarcasm and teasing to heart. It undermines their sense of competence and makes them feel unsafe. Using sarcasm, insults, or humiliation about our kids' feelings definitely insures that in the future we won't hear about how they really feel. If they can't trust their parents when they feel good or bad, whom can they trust?

Another strategy that never helps is denying the importance of feelings. Louise's son Aaron came home one day in tears—he wanted a starring role in the sixth-grade play but was only picked for the chorus. "It's not such a big deal," Louise said. "You have a part, even if it's not the one you wanted. Think how bad you'd feel if you didn't get any part at all."

Louise was trying to comfort Aaron, but her words backfired: he started wondering what was wrong with him. If "it was no big deal," why did he feel so bad?

Look at your own emotions

To be an emotion coach, it helps to look at how we think about and handle our own feelings. Ask yourself these questions:

- Do you fly off the handle and curse a driver who cuts you off on the highway or do you shrug it off?
- How do you calm yourself down? Do you spend time by yourself? Talk to your spouse or a friend?
- If you didn't get the promotion you counted on, would you keep your sadness and disappointment inside or share your feelings with your family?
- Can you listen to a friend describe feeling sad without trying to "make it better"?
- Do you want to hear about emotions like love and happiness but get uncomfortable when people are sad or angry?

Parents can't be effective coaches to their children if they don't think about how they handle emotions themselves. ❑

When Your Child Sulks, Whines, Complains, Or Is Grouchy

Joan Tyler's nine-year-old son, Frank, has a certain hair-raising way of wailing her name: he drags out "mom" so it has about ten syllables. Every parent knows that high-pitched whiny tone. Whether it emanates from a five-year-old or a preteen, at home or in front of a crowd at the supermarket, it's as grating to parental nerves as fingernails on a blackboard—just as kids' constant complaints are. Like most of us, Joan feels like shouting "Snap out of it!" to make these irritating behaviors stop.

We're all tempted to believe that our kids are whiny or grumpy just to spite us, but no matter how badly your child's complaints get under your skin, try to remember he's acting that way for a reason, not just to drive you crazy. It's more accurate—and productive—to assume that your child is trying to communicate some emotional or physical need. Finding out what it is will help you stop the behavior.

Common causes of whines and sulks

Many kids, especially younger ones, whine when they are tired or sick, and the best cure is prevention. For others, whining is an unpleasant and habitual bid for attention. In that case the solution is to teach them other ways to ask for it—and consistently insist that they do!

Though a sulky child is quiet and withdrawn while a whiner takes every opportunity to let you know exactly how bad she feels, often both are suffering from the same problem: something left unresolved.

Set aside special "mope" time

Seven-year-old Breann stalked off to her room to sulk after her mom said she couldn't go Rollerblading with a friend because they hadn't yet replaced her lost kneepads. Other friends called, but Breann wouldn't talk to them. Like kids who whine in similar situations, she couldn't let go of her disappointment. Her well-intentioned mom tried to hurry Breann out of her mood, but by not letting her daughter talk about how disappointed she was, Breann's mom prolonged it.

Finally she said, "I know you're disappointed not to go Rollerblading. I'm going to give you a full hour to sulk and feel as

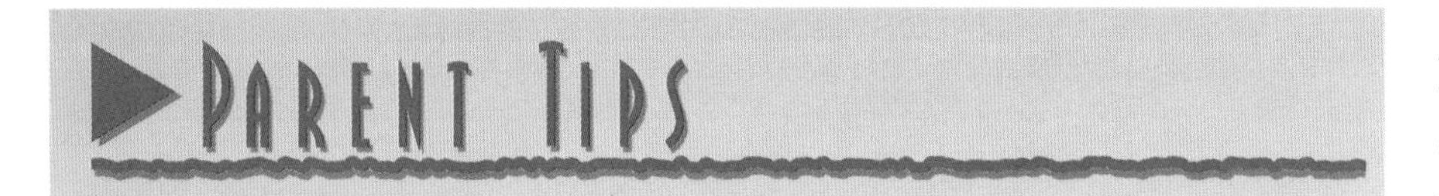

- "Our 10-year-old, Elaine, complained about having to practice the piano 20 minutes a day. Finally we told her to write down 3 reasons why she shouldn't take lessons. She came up with 25 hilarious ones, including 'To protect your eardrums!' We laughed and compromised: she'd practice 10 minutes a day. Then most of her whining stopped," says Ezra, father of 2.
- "Sam's whining was a habit—he hardly realized when he was doing it! Finally I set a limit and told him that if he whined more than 3 times for something he wouldn't get it at all," reports Ann, mother of a 6-year-old.

bad as you want. That's your job. I don't want you to do anything else. When the timer rings, though, that job is over." As it turns out, an hour is a long time to sulk. Breann was out of her room in fifteen minutes, feeling better.

Remember though, when children sulk after disagreements with friends, they often do this as a form of self-protection—it's easier to retreat to their room than risk getting hurt again.

Complainers and grouches

Like Oscar, the popular grouch from PBS's *Sesame Street*, grouchy kids manage to see the unhappy side of situations and find fault with everything: the bath water is too cold, the Coke is warm, the jeans don't fit right, a friend always does better on tests, parents love a little sister more than they do her. Living with a perpetually dissatisfied child is a terrible strain. After spending considerable time trying to figure out how can they make things right, parents quite understandably become annoyed. But this only muddies the waters.

Take a temperamental inventory

First, stop trying to make everything okay. Then look at your child's temperament (see pages 20-21). Maybe many of the whines or complaints, particularly those about clothing, food, temperature, and sound are a result of a low sensory threshold. Greg, for example, constantly complained that he was hot and sweaty. His mom finally realized that he was sensitive to polyester clothing. Once she began buying cotton shirts and pants, his complaints stopped.

Look for patterns

If complaints and grouchiness seem more general, try keeping very careful track of them—even when you feel like tuning them out. Do they increase at a particular time of day? Are they about friends more than anything else? School? A sibling? Is your child grouchiest when it's time to shift from one activity to the next? Try to find a common thread, and then address the problem by talking with your child.

Put kids in control

Often children complain the most about issues over which they feel they have no control. What helps is finding ways in which they can make even small decisions. My friend Marcie realized that most of her twelve-year-old son's complaints were about his younger brother's encroachment on his territory, so she asked him to come up with suggestions to resolve the problem. After some thought, Don decided to place his CD player, CDs, and several special video games off-limits to his brother. Because he came up with this solution himself, he felt more in control and stopped complaining, at least a little. ❑

Why do kids get grouchy?

- "When I call my friends but no one can play, or when it's raining and I can't play outside," says Molly, 7.
- "When my friends make crazy demands on me, like I have to always compliment them on their clothes, but they never compliment me," reports Margi, 11.
- "When I stay up too late watching TV and then sleep too late," says Hank, 13.

When Your Child Gets Frustrated

Frustration is what everyone feels when they can't reach a goal, obtain something they want, or accomplish what they've set out to do because obstacles, setbacks, or interruptions get in their way. Six-year-old Kevin, for example, has been trying to build a tall tower with blocks. But every time he gets to level eight, it collapses. Eventually he becomes so frustrated he throws a block across the room.

Or take thirteen-year-old Rona, who erupts into tears when her dad inquires how her report on the Civil War is coming. "It's due in three days," she shrieks, "and I'll never get it done! It's so unfair. The teacher didn't tell us what to do."

The result of feeling frustrated is often anger, especially when children feel a situation is unfair. Though all kids feel this way from time to time, some of them seem to get frustrated so much more easily than others do. Why?

Responses to frustration differ

Some children are born with a lower tolerance for frustration and they tend to give up at the first sign of difficulty. Persistent kids, on the other hand, expect setbacks as well as success and keep going. We can give easily frustrated kids a boost by first helping them calm down, and then by showing them how to create several smaller steps toward their goal. That way they have more chances to experience success along the way. We also need to understand that frustration has a way of building up till kids snap. After a day of coping with first grade and a playdate, a collapsed tower was the last straw for Kevin!

Refocus attention

Kids also grow frustrated when they can't learn how to do something like read, ride a bike, skateboard, Rollerblade, or ice skate as quickly as they want to. What helps? Refocus their attention on the process of learning and celebrate any small step of progress, as Lynn did when her son was trying to learn to ride a bike. She told him, "You know, just a month ago, you wouldn't have been able to ride this far even with training wheels on your bike. If you keep practicing, you'll be riding down the entire block in no time."

Children are also encouraged by hearing how hard it was for us to learn something. When Robbie was learning to ice skate, his dad reminded him that he hadn't learned to skate until he was 18! Robbie couldn't believe what a klutz his father was—and that made him feel a lot better.

Know when to intervene

As schoolwork becomes more complex and demanding, academic performance becomes an issue. Kids often grow frustrated when they have difficulty with homework or when their achievement on tests and report cards doesn't live up to their expectations. Sometimes these are unrealistic, like thinking they can memorize fifty spelling words in one night, and then we have to gently bring them in line with reality. Sometimes kids need help with required skills. Rona's dad realized she didn't know how to research a paper, so he showed her how to find reference books at the library and, later, how to make an outline.

The most effective way to minimize kids' frustration at school is to stay involved. James complained and complained that fifth-grade math was too hard. By the time his mom met with the teacher, she learned he was way behind. A tutor helped him catch up—and ended James' frustration with fractions. Some kids who are chronically frustrated by schoolwork turn out to have learning disabilities.

"Don't fence me in"

The biggest source of frustration for kids in junior high school? Easy—their parents. By insisting on curfews and adult supervision at parties, we seem to be standing between them and a good time. They pine for a limit-free life—or so they say.

In reality, they not only want limits but need them. If they're included in the decision-making process, however, they find our limits much less frustrating. Rather than imposing a curfew on his thirteen-year-old son, Alex's father asks *him* to come up with a time.

"What about midnight?" Alex says.

"That's a little too late for me to feel comfortable," his dad replies. "Ten-thirty?"

"I don't want to always be the first one to leave. How about eleven?"

"Eleven's fine—for tonight."

Not only will negotiation cut down on your child's frustration, it also helps ensure that he'll get home on time. ❑

❍ "I get frustrated when I have too much homework on a night when I have baseball practice. So first I make a plan, then I say to myself, 'Just stay calm.' I turn the clock to the wall so I won't worry about how long it takes to do my math," says Samuel, 10.

When Your Child Is Angry

"I'm never playing with Matthew again," Jon shouts to his mom as he thunders into the kitchen, throws his baseball glove across the room, and kicks the door so hard she can feel the glass vibrating. "He always has to win, always . . ."

Meanwhile, next door at the McCalls' house, screams drift down from the upstairs. The subsequent conversation goes like this:

"Dad, Mona pulled my hair."

"It's not my fault, Dad. I had to! Kerry borrowed my best shirt without asking and spilled something on it!"

At the Hills' house, Lisa comes home from school with a stormy face. "Don't talk to me. I hate all adults," she retorts when her dad inquires what's wrong.

Most parents see and hear these faces and sounds of anger in their kids much more than they want to. In fact, this difficult but common emotion is the one we most often try to stifle, probably because angry kids often make their parents angry! We forget that helping kids manage their anger starts with acknowledging it. Only then can we help them cool down, understand what triggered their feelings, and use this information to make positive changes.

Accept feelings but set limits

When our kids are mad they feel like Jon—as though they're in a pressure cooker and they have to do something dramatic or they'll explode. Psychologists call anger an "enabling" emotion because when we're angry, we have plenty of energy for action. The most valuable lesson about anger we can teach children—and it's never too early to start—is that having angry feelings doesn't mean they have to act them out in destructive ways by yelling, breaking something, or hitting or hurting someone else or themselves.

The best way to do this is to stay calm and set limits, the way Jon's mom did. She told him, "I know you're angry at Matt, but it's not okay to storm into the house and kick and throw things when you lose your temper." Similarly, Lisa's dad told her, "I can see that you're angry, but it makes me mad when you take it out on me."

Kids whose parents set limits and enforce them are less likely to act out aggressively when they're angry at school or with friends. If kids still punch and kick at the age of nine or regularly bully others, their anger is out of control and they need professional help (see pages 85-86).

What's okay?

To help kids use their anger constructively, we have to help them learn to transmute it into positive actions instead of pursuing dreams of retaliation. I advise my kids to use words to say how they feel and why, to me or to the person who made them angry. For my nine-year-old son, Jake, just admitting his anger helps dissipate it. I try to get

AGE FACTOR

❖ By the age of 5, most children have outgrown knock-down, drag-out tantrums—but some 5- and 6-year-olds still have them. They are still impulsive and are easily frustrated by the gap between their abilities and their desires.

Kids this age also feel very competitive with each other, and often throw tantrums when they feel upstaged in school or on the playground.

him to stop talking about the person he's upset with and focus on himself. "You bet I'm angry," he says, usually realizing, as he says it, that he's beginning to feel slightly calmer.

Some kids need a physical outlet for the energy set in motion by anger, such as shooting baskets over and over or running as fast as they can. Six-year-old Amy draws a picture of how she feels, then crosses it out, crumples it up, and throws it out. In the past fifteen years, researchers have found it's important to channel angry energy in positive, not aggressive, ways. They no longer recommend kids pound on a pillow, pretending it's the person they're mad at to get rid of anger. It turns out that such aggressive actions lead to more rage!

Keep in mind that even though both boys and girls are equally likely to get angry, parents more often convey the message that anger is bad to girls. Parents still tolerate angry behavior in sons more than they do in daughters.

Take a time-out

Trying to discuss a situation rationally with kids when their anger is at its peak is a big mistake. Instead, tell them, as Jon's mom did, "Take fifteen minutes in your room to calm down, and then come and tell me what happened." While this time-out method is very effective with most children, it doesn't work for everyone. My son Ben felt as if he was being exiled to his room when he was younger. "Stay with me," he would plead. "Help me calm down." Eventually, I realized that he honestly didn't know what he was supposed to do during the time-out. The idea of being alone with his rage terrified him.

Teach kids how to calm down

Many kids, no matter what their ages, simply don't know how to calm themselves down and need parents to teach them. Counting to ten or one hundred, taking several deep breaths, and saying something quiet and encouraging to yourself, such as "Everything will turn out okay in the end," are three tried-and-true methods to use.

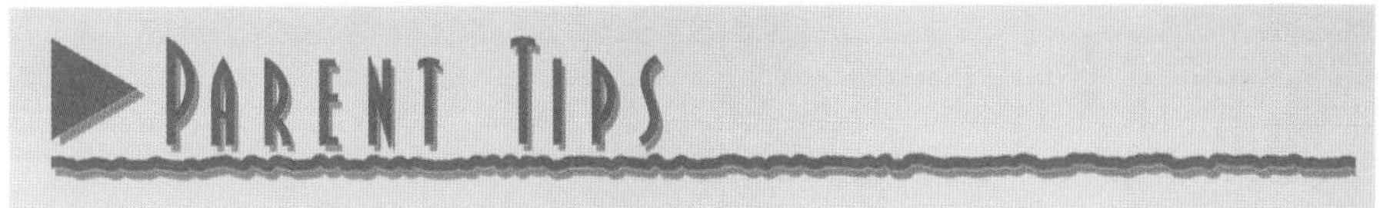

What to do about anger in public:

- "My kids always seem to get angry at me or each other in supermarkets, libraries, malls, stores, or restaurants. When tempers flare and I sense that things are about to escalate, I drop everything and take them outside," says Jane, mother of 2 girls.
- "I've learned not to worry about what other people are thinking when my kids lose their cool outside the house. I assume everyone who's a parent has been there. Instead, I just try to help my boys calm down," says Joe, father of 2 boys.

DID YOU KNOW?

Research has shown that several reactions to anger are not effective. When children are angry, don't:

- ignore their feelings
- punish them
- humiliate them, by saying "You're too old to act this way"
- say something sarcastic, as in "You look so attractive when you get angry"

Meditation is even more effective. I taught my son on an afternoon when we had nothing much to do. We sat on the floor, legs crossed, and closed our eyes. I told him to inhale deeply through his nose, then exhale forcefully through his mouth while he pictured a peaceful scene. His choice was the shore of the lake by his grandparents' house. Soon he could concentrate on how his breath moved through his body and notice how much calmer and more relaxed he felt.

The next time he was angry, he used the meditation method in his room, and gradually his agitation drained away.

We all know that some kids get angrier than others. Hot-tempered, impulsive, intense, and excitable kids have great difficulty calming down and curbing their aggression when angry. For these kids, it's important to use every opportunity to practice, practice, practice!

Find the cause and anticipate

The truth is, anger is usually understandable. Among school-aged kids the trigger is frequently a conflict with a friend, a teacher, or a sibling. What do you do when your sister grabs the last cookie or a friend pushes you in the cafeteria? What else can you do besides get mad? Reviewing an angry situation helps kids consider how they could have reacted differently and figure out ways to prevent an over-the-top angry outburst from occurring in the future. David, for example, realized Todd provoked him every time they stood together in the cafeteria line, so he simply decided to stand with a different friend.

Often less assertive kids get angry because they don't know how to tell friends or siblings calmly that they don't like what they are doing or saying. Mona might not have felt so angry at her sister if she had been able to say, "Kerry, I feel upset that you took my shirt without asking, and then spilled something on it. I expect you to get it cleaned for me."

How we interpret a situation affects how we feel and react. A review helps kids look at something in a different light. After Jon's mom sympathized with his feelings, she encouraged him to recall what Matt had done to make him angry by asking "Did Matt cheat? Or was he just trying his very hardest to win?" Jon realized that he was mad because Matt wanted to quit playing right after Matt had made a home run.

Researchers also believe that coming up with a new understanding of why a person angered us is an effective way to handle our angry feelings.

Put it in perspective

One way adults soothe their anger is by reminding themselves of the good side of a situation. We can coach kids in this strategy, as Lisa's dad did. Lisa explained to him,

"I was mad
because of my science teacher!
I was late to class—it wasn't my fault—and he humiliated me by making me sit up front and answer every question."

"Well, did you know the answers to the questions?" her dad asked.

"Most of them," Lisa replied.

"Then his plan backfired, didn't it? You didn't embarrass yourself at all; quite the contrary."

"I guess," Lisa admitted. With her dad's help, she'd found a way to make herself feel better—and less angry—about what had happened.

With ingenuity we can help kids see the silver lining in many angry situations. If a first grader has a mini-tantrum because she can't tie her shoes, we can help her put her frustration in perspective by saying, "Even though you didn't tie your shoes, you worked on it a long time. You have great perseverance!"

When your child is angry at you

First of all, don't take it too personally. Children are frequently angry with their parents, and sometimes they're right to be (see pages 56-57). I use these times to help my children—and myself—notice the physical signs that they're growing hot under the collar. I point out the way their hearts beat faster, their cheeks turn red, their breath becomes shallow. If we learn to notice these warning signs, we can short-circuit fights before they erupt by saying something like, "I'm getting angry, so I'm going into the other room before I say something I'll regret." Practicing this at home helps kids use the same technique at school and in conflicts with friends. ❑

When Your Child Says, "I Hate You!"

I'll never forget the first time my oldest son, then about six, screwed up his face, already contorted in anger because I wouldn't buy him a new action figure, and spat out the words, "I hate you, Mom."

I felt the mixture of emotions most parents do. Part of me was tempted to laugh because I knew he didn't mean it—he was parroting something he'd heard from his friends. But another part of me was crying and upset. How could my son, whom I loved so dearly, say he despised me? At the same time, I recognized how brave it was. There he was, a little pipsqueak, standing up to his powerful mom. Announcing that he hated me was his way of serving me notice that he was separate enough to fight on a more grown-up level and felt secure enough to show me the full force of his fury, in a way I never could as a child.

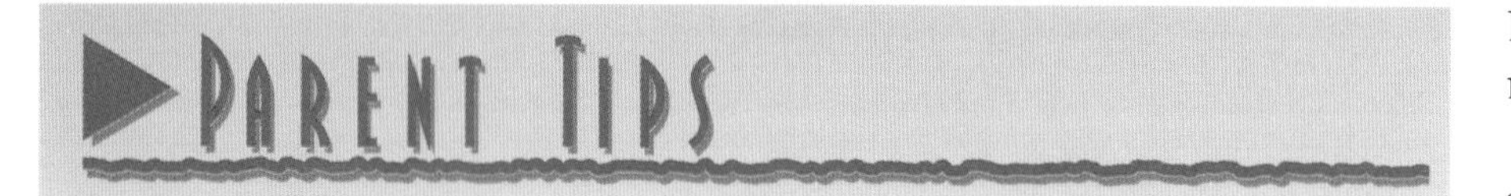

- "Often when Helene says, 'I hate you!' she's angry because she thinks I've let her down in some way. If I failed to do something for her that I said I would, I apologize and tell her, 'Hey, I'm not perfect either!'" explains Phyllis, mother of a 10-year-old.
- "I was hurt when my 12-year-old started calling me a 'hypocrite.' Talking with my sister, who has 3 teens, gave me some perspective. Now I try to think back to what I said to my parents!" says Abe, father of a boy.

"I hate you!" is just the first of many personal zingers our kids throw when they're angry with us. As they grow from ages five to thirteen, most of us hear any number of them, such as: "You always say no!" "Dad (or Mom) is nicer than you are!" "You're so unfair!" "You're such a hypocrite." It's worth remembering that one way kids and especially adolescents develop is by arguing and defying us, sometimes using withering scorn.

Don't overreact

Though it's very hard not to boil over at moments like these, the best way to weather our children's expressions of hatred and anger toward us is to take a deep breath or two or even three, and not allow ourselves to get drawn into an on-the-spot protracted argument. Focus on the emotions, not the words, and stay calm.

"I know that you're very angry at me," I told my son. "We'll talk about it, but not right now. Let's wait until you're calmer."

It's important that kids hear you acknowledge their underlying feelings without trying to contradict or deny them, experts advise. To say, "You don't really hate me" or "I'm not being unfair" flies in the face of their own perceptions and feelings at that moment. At the same time, we do our kids a favor by helping them realize that erupting angrily and personally during an argument isn't appropriate.

Air grievances

The timing of follow-up discussions is also important. You don't want to wait too long! Try to gauge how long it takes for your child—and you—to return to some kind of emotional equilibrium. "I know I can approach my son after a blowup when I hear him humming in his room," observes Sheila, eight-year-old Jonah's mom. "If he's still angry, he's conspicuously silent."

Once you sit down to talk, forget personal feelings and think of the discussion as a fact-finding mission. "I focus on asking questions and listening," says Lila, mother of eleven-year-old Marta. "I want to get her talking about what's bothering her, what I did that made her so angry. I have to work extra hard at not being defensive when she accuses me of purposely trying to ruin her life by not letting her go to the mall, though she knew she shouldn't go—she had a test the next day. But I just nod. From her perspective, it was my fault. I can explain my view at a later time."

Lila has also learned that if she interrupts her daughter during a gripe session, Marta, like most kids, ends up feeling frustrated all over again.

Ask for their ideas

Swing into action only after your child has aired the entire list of grievances, advises Lila. She asks, "What can we do to make sure we don't have this fight again?" By asking your child to come up with a specific solution, you're putting the ball in her court. Not only does she feel you value her opinion, but she has the challenge of coming up with something that will make her feel better.

Remember, too, that our kids' gripes are sometimes justified. Parents do promise to buy something and then renege, impose unrealistic expectations, or blame the kids for something they didn't do.

Usually our children's requests for a change prove easy to comply with. Evelyn's seven-year-old son complained that he hated it when she talked on the phone after dinner because he wanted her to be available for help when he did his homework. She realized she could make her calls later and rearranged her schedule to accommodate his wishes.

End with love

It's also comforting for kids to hear that we all have feelings of intense anger, even hatred, but that these are natural and don't last long. "Even when I'm angry at you I still love you," I told my sons when they were little, and they still repeat this back to me after our fights. I see that they feel reassured. Violent emotions leave everyone feeling tempest-tossed, and kids of all ages need to be reminded that once the storm abates, they'll find themselves in a harbor where they are safe and loved. ❑

ASK THE EXPERTS

- **"Even under the best of circumstances, an angry child can make a parent feel angry. . . It's also common for parents' anger at children to run the gamut from mild irritation to murderous, if fleeting, fantasies," writes psychiatrist Henry A. Paul, Executive Director of the Karen Horney Clinic, in his book, *When Kids Are Mad, Not Bad.***

About Jealousy & Envy

Here's an easy way to distinguish between the two: kids feel envious of things they don't have, and jealous about the ones they have but are afraid of losing to someone else. Ten-year-old Mark is envious of the mountain bike his friend Ron received for his birthday because he doesn't have one, but he's jealous of his new baby sister because he's afraid his parents now love her more than him.

Shakespeare called jealousy "the green-eye'd monster." It's a difficult emotion—hard to admit to, hard to handle. Yet it's as common as love and hate; in fact, it's a subtle blend of both, with a dash of sadness, anger, and frustration thrown in.

Why kids get jealous of siblings

If you have more than one child, you have at least some jealousy, resentment, and rivalry in your household. Kids are always sure a brother or sister is getting an inch more lemonade, more—and better—presents, or the most chances to pick what to watch on TV. But the real reason siblings get so jealous of each other is because each one fears there's not enough love and parental attention to go around—and that he or she will be on the losing end.

Surprisingly, some researchers report that the bigger the family, the less jealousy among the siblings because younger siblings also rely on their older brothers and sisters for support and love.

Cutting down on sibling jealousy

Most children like to be asked how they feel about becoming a big sister or brother and are less jealous if they know what to expect before the baby is born. Enrolling them in a prenatal class for siblings (now offered by many hospitals) where they can learn to diaper and hold a baby helps, as does involving them in the baby's care, even in token ways. In fact, according to the latest studies, the more time an older sibling spends with the baby, the less hostile he or she will feel toward the baby.

But the most effective cure for jealousy with siblings of all ages is giving each child a one-on-one time of at least fifteen minutes every day and a chance to feel special. One family allows each child a weekly VIP day on which he or she gets the first helping of dessert and the choice of what to watch on TV. In another, each child goes out for dinner once a month with a parent. Most parents find they have to remind children that acting on jealous feelings in mean ways is never acceptable. Posting rules for how to treat one another helps. Don't be surprised if friction increases when one child is in middle school; about twenty percent of these kids say they get along "badly" with younger siblings.

How parents contribute

We can also recognize and correct the ways many of us subtly but unwittingly encourage

DID YOU KNOW?

- First-borns, especially boys, express more distress, ambivalence, and hostility about their siblings.
- Mother-daughter relationships are more affected by the birth of a new baby than mother-son relationships.
- The majority of older siblings commonly react to a new baby with negativism, withdrawal, and sleep problems, but most of these problems disappear after about 8 months.
- In one study, the more amiable and easy-going the new baby was, the less hostility and jealousy siblings expressed.

siblings to be jealous. Making comparisons with remarks like "Too bad your report card didn't resemble your brother's" or "Melinda is clearly the best athlete in this family" fans the flames. Instead try to concentrate on the uniqueness of each child and mention it to him or her often.

When the problem is a new mate

Kids often feel jealous of a single parent's new mate, too. Whether a person has become a regular date or a new spouse, many children worry that their parent will have less time for them and love them less. Make sure you emphasize your continuing love to them, involve them in any plans (such as an upcoming wedding), and set aside some special times to be alone together.

Jealousy between friends

Jealousy in friendships begins to blossom when children start having best friends, especially among girls in the third, fourth, and fifth grades. Suddenly kids start worrying about losing a close friend, and they become very possessive, the way Leann did when she began middle school and her best friend since first grade started spending time with another girl. Leann felt heartbroken and rejected. Her mom sympathized with how hard it was for her daughter to share her friend. But she also used the opportunity to talk to Leann about what it means to be a friend, consider why her friend was branching out, and encourage *her* to approach other girls.

What about envy?

All children feel envious at times, wishing they'd won the spelling bee or had curly hair like the girl down the street. Problems arise when kids hurt others to feel better about themselves. It's never pleasant to discover your own wonderful child is picking on or spreading gossip about a friend out of envy. Yet this happens. That's when we need to let kids know that it's natural to feel bad they didn't win the spelling bee and to want to strike out at someone, but hurting someone else won't change who won. One mom reminds her son that it's easy to be kind and generous when everything goes your way, but she'll be especially proud of him when he's generous to a friend who won the trophy he wanted. ❑

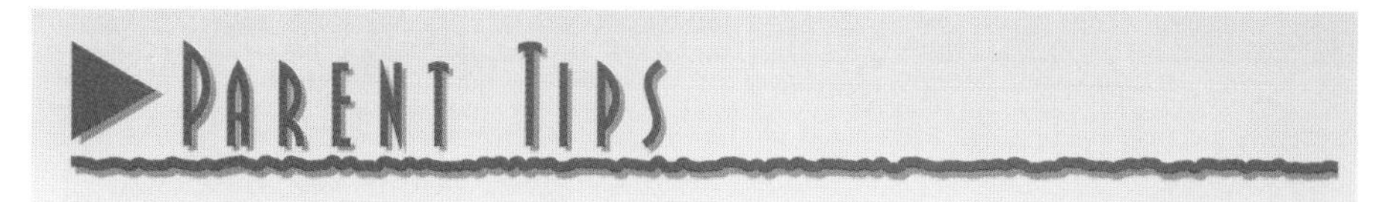

- "Jealousy loves company. My 13-year-old daughter couldn't stop crying when the boy she liked asked another girl to the school dance—until I told her that the same thing happened to me at 13. She wanted to know every detail, and soon we were laughing about how one day she would console her daughter the same way," says Ruth, mother of 2 girls.

About Moping, Blue Moods, & Sadness

At Gail's sixth birthday party, one of the guests was nearing meltdown. She didn't win at any of the games, the T-shirt she colored came out all wrong, and when she didn't get the piece of cake she wanted, she burst into heartbroken tears. Everyone froze. A split second later, her dad appeared to whisk her away from the table. "That's all right," he said to his daughter as they sat together on the couch, and he stroked her hair. "Just go ahead and cry."

The art of comforting

Have you ever heard more comforting words? This wise dad didn't try to make it better: he didn't mug funny faces or tell jokes to distract his daughter; he didn't say things like "It's not so bad" or "You're at a birthday party, you're not supposed to feel sad." He just let her cry her heart out.

Isn't that what we all want to hear when we're sad? We don't want to dry our eyes or cheer up or think of all the terrible things that haven't happened or of all the great things that will happen tomorrow. We just want to sit and feel sad—not forever, just for a few minutes. Often that's all it takes for our kids' sadness to pack its bags and leave. Yet because seeing kids sad is so unsettling to most of us, we usually feel as if we should do something—which often makes things worse. The key to dealing with children's sadness is to say and do less, and listen more carefully.

Feeling blue

Unfortunately, not all kids' sad feelings vanish after a good cry and a hug. Blue moods can linger, and once they take hold, they are sometimes hard to shake.

Children suffer many very real losses that can cause long-lasting sadness, and some of them are not the obvious ones. These days, for example, my younger son is mourning the fact that his beloved older brother, nearing sixteen, wants less and less to do with him. "Ben used to want to play with me sometimes," he says, his eyes brimming with tears. "Now he doesn't want to play with me at all."

The best I can do for Jake is be aware of how he feels and make myself available when he wants to talk about it. Sometimes he doesn't want to say anything; we simply sit together quietly.

Age-old comfort still helps

Stories also have the power to make kids feel better, especially when they are stories of parents' experiences. I tell Jake how my sister felt similarly deserted by me when I began high school, but as adults we are growing ever closer. This doesn't always happen, I say, but it happened to me, and it could happen to you and your brother, too. This story has taken on a fairy-tale quality for Jake, and he requests it often.

The age-old sayings many of us often resort to when we're feeling low, such as

AGE FACTOR

❖ A recent study found that boys feel depressed more often than girls *before* age 13, but girls report feeling depressed almost twice as much as boys *after* age 13. The degree to which girls—but not boys—feel emotionally supported by their moms seems to be a factor in how depressed they feel.

"Time heals all wounds" or "You'll make new friends," help kids, too, as they did seven-year-old Deanne. She was devastated when her cousins moved across the country. "Now they can't come over for holidays or my birthday," she wailed to her mom, Anita.

"Maybe we can plan a trip to visit them during summer vacation," Anita offered. Then she reminded her daughter that the love between the cousins would endure despite the distance. "Remember, you always have your cousins in your heart," she told Deanne, "where you can visit with them any time you want." Children are very receptive to these kinds of hopeful statements from parents—as long as we believe the advice we're offering.

Break the taboo of silence

In many families, parents are sometimes hesitant to bring up relatives who have died or other sad situations. How should I broach the subject? they wonder—and then assume they don't have to, since their children aren't asking questions.

But just because your son isn't talking about his grandma who recently died, his friend who moved away, or his dog who was run over doesn't mean he isn't thinking about them. In fact, he probably wishes that *he* knew how to start such a conversation with you.

Fortunately, there are many naturally occurring opportunities. There may be a story in the newspaper about a child whose beloved pet was run over that you can read to your child. You can find books that deal with a specific loss or choose a video about a grandparent who becomes ill or dies to

ASK THE EXPERTS

According to Dr. Janice Zeman of the University of Maine:

- **Boys are less likely to talk about their sad feelings than girls because they expect parents to react negatively.**
- **Both boys and girls feel more comfortable talking about their sad feelings to their mothers than their fathers.**
- **Girls are more comfortable expressing sadness than anger.**

- "When I get sad, I go into my nest. I take all the pillows off the couch and stack them behind a certain chair by a corner, and I lie down and take deep breaths," says Deirdre, 11.

- "I get sad when I don't have anyone to play with. So I go into my room and take out a special set of action figures that I only play with by myself," says Thomas, 6.

generate discussion about Grandpa Joe. If your child seems eager to talk, then he's grateful that you gave him the chance.

Talk about your own sadness

As adults, we tend to keep sadness to ourselves because we don't want to burden children with our pain, nor do we want our sadness to overwhelm them. So we save our tears for private moments. But if we always grieve behind closed doors, we deprive our kids of the opportunity to see that sadness is a feeling we all experience, and that there are ways to cope with it.

"One of my oldest friends was diagnosed with cancer," says Stella, "and my thirteen-year-old daughter came home and found me in tears. Penny asked what was wrong. I didn't give her all the gory details, but I explained that a good friend of mine was very sick, and I was very sad about it."

Penny nodded and went up to her room. Stella was afraid that she'd overwhelmed her daughter. But that night, before bed, Penny told her mother that she was very sorry about her friend, and that she hoped things would be all right.

If we don't show our kids that sadness is part of our emotional palette, they won't feel entitled to their own sad feelings.

Helping brooders

Remember Charlie Brown, from the comic strip "Peanuts," who walked around with a dark cloud directly over his head? That's how it feels when a blue mood settles on us. If kids can't shake their sadness despite our attempts at comfort and conversation, then they may be upset about something we're not aware of. Too often we assume that we know what's troubling our kids, when in fact we're completely off base.

That's what happened when Bobby's grandfather died. His parents assumed that Bobby was sad because of that. It turned out that Bobby was also sad that the family had to cut short their vacation to return home for the funeral, fairly normal for a child only six years old. But until his parents asked him what he was sad about, they weren't treating all the causes.

Brainstorm for solutions

Bobby's parents enlisted his help. "I understand that you were very sad that we had to come home early from the beach because Grandpa got sick," his mom said. "What do you think would help you feel better?" Most children love being consulted. Bobby thought for a while, and then said that he'd like to spend a day at a local amusement and water park. Soon his brooding lifted.

If your child has trouble coming up with a suggestion, help him brainstorm—throw out lots of ideas and see which one appeals. Or you can tell your child to think about it, and promise that you'll talk about it later. The fact that you took the time to solicit his opinion will go a long way toward dissipating broodiness.

Respecting privacy

As children grow, however, they become less willing to talk about their feelings, particularly sadness, because it makes them feel vulnerable. By the time they reach middle school, their insatiable quest for privacy makes conversation more difficult.

"'Leave me alone,' that's all I hear from my daughter," says Suzanne, mother of twelve-year-old Alison. "She doesn't want to talk about it, even when I know she's feeling sad she wasn't invited to a particular party. She just wants to mope around the house." In fact, moody adolescents sometimes need time to do just that without our interference. But if you're worried about a close-mouthed preteen, try playing a version of the game Categories. My friend asks her son to identify whether what's making him so blue is related to schoolwork, a teacher, a friend, a girl, or the family. Once he identifies the category, she asks if the problem is something he feels he can handle on his own, if he'd like her help, or if he wants to talk to a counselor at school or a trusted aunt or uncle.

"This way," my friend explains, "I feel as if my son knows that I'm interested in his well-being but trusts that I won't intrude. Once he starts talking, he often can't stop, and ends up telling me what's wrong."

When sadness becomes depression

Sadness is fairly straightforward; depression is much more complicated and serious (see pages 32-35). Not every extended blue mood turns into depression, but parents need to be on the lookout for any of the following warning signs.

Depression interferes with a child's functioning, causing changes in appetite, sleep, personal hygiene, and behavior. For example, if your child begins retreating to his room right after school, refuses phone calls, and sleeps a lot after school and on weekends, these are red flags. Also be alert for statements like "I'm no good at anything" or "What's the use of trying?" If these continue for more than several weeks, consult your pediatrician. Depression needs immediate attention. ❑

▶ Parent Tips

- "I sit with my son in his closet when he's sad. He likes the darkness, but he needs me to be with him," says Frances, mother of a 5-year-old.
- "When I notice that Lucy seems down in the dumps, we leaf through magazines together. I look for pictures that involve loss or disappointment and use these to draw her out," explains Hugh, father of 2 girls.

About Hurt Feelings & Being Too Sensitive

Sometimes it seems that eight-year-old Alice gets upset if other kids even look cross-eyed at her. Her mom observed worriedly, "She has the thinnest skin of any child I've ever seen."

Our kids get a rude awakening as they move from the protected world of their parents and caretakers to the rough-and-tumble atmosphere of school. Super-sensitive children like Alice remind us of a painful reality that all kids encounter from time to time—that feeling hurt is an inevitable part of growing up, learning to get along, and having friends. For kids ages five to thirteen, their world outside the family is shaped by their relationships with other kids, and teasing and feeling left out are a big source of their hurt feelings.

Children with high self-esteem and a temperamental inclination to roll with the punches quickly develop a tough hide that protects them somewhat, but others, like Alice, do not.

AGE FACTOR

- In 1st grade, boys and girls are equally likely to express pain.
- By 5th grade, however, boys are much less likely to express sadness and pain than girls.
- The change for boys begins around 3rd grade.

Replay the scene

Some sensitive kids blow ordinary encounters out of proportion, perceiving slights or rejections where none are intended. That was the case with seven-year-old Alan, who often came home complaining that Joe (or Nate or Andy) had hurt his feelings. As a reality check, his mom began listening in when he played with friends. One afternoon, his friend Richie wanted to play video games, but Alan wanted to ride bikes. "You always want to ride bikes, so you must be a bike maniac," Richie said. Pleased with his joke, he kept calling Alan that all afternoon as they rode around the neighborhood.

Later, when Alan told his mom that being called names like "maniac" annoyed him and hurt his feelings, she helped him reevaluate Richie's remark. "Do you think he was calling you that in a mean way?" she asked. "I thought he was just making a friendly joke."

Replaying a scene and asking about the other child's intentions, as Alan's mom did, helps kids think about what happened in a different, and often more realistic, way. In many instances kids end up deciding, "I guess the teasing wasn't as bad as I thought it was." Alan's mom also pointed out an important social truth: that kids usually like to joke around with the people they like and feel comfortable with.

Helping kids develop a sense of humor about these situations is important, too.

Taking charge

There are other times when hurt feelings result from serious rejection or teasing. And sometimes kids are tagged "overly sensitive" precisely because their perceptions of what's going on *are* so accurate. What another child brushes off, they take to heart because they're aware of the mean intention beneath it. But doing nothing makes overly sensitive kids feel powerless and perpetuates the hurt feelings.

Becky, for example, was teased about her freckles and her curly red hair. No matter how she combed it, by mid-morning curls were sticking out. She was beginning to feel bad about how she looked—an area in which many kids are sensitive. What hurt most, her dad discovered, was being singled out for looking different.

After brainstorming, she came up with a rejoinder to try when kids teased: "You know, you're right. I have very crazy hair. It just won't listen to me." When she finally used it at school, the teasing subsided—and so did her hurt feelings. If your child's efforts don't work, however, ask his or her teacher for help.

The overly sensitive preteen

By the time children reach the age of eleven, their sensitivity is often so finely tuned that it seems as if no one, even parents, can breathe without their feeling wounded. Corrine's solution is to remind her thirteen-year-old son at every opportunity that she felt the same way when she was his age, that all his friends feel the same way, and that these feelings will pass. She also reassures him that in the meantime, his family loves him very much.

Don't overprotect!

It's never pleasant to see our kids hurt, especially when we know they're very sensitive! Many of us find it hard not to be protective and rush in to solve the problem for them. But that doesn't help children, supersensitive or not, in the long run. To develop a tougher skin so they can take hurts in stride, our kids need encouragement and help to handle them on their own. ❑

- "When a kid hurts my feelings, I try to think of him doing something embarrassing, like using baby talk when he's talking to the teacher," says Dan, 9.
- "What hurts my feelings is when I call a friend and she doesn't want to play with me. So what I do is hang up and then pretend she's still on the line, and I say out loud, 'Maybe next time you'll want to come over.' I really think she will," says Jane, 7.

When Your Child Feels Like A Failure

In contrast to the loud fury of anger, our children's admissions of failure are usually quiet, almost mumbled. One afternoon Ezra, who's ten, came home from school looking completely discouraged. He slowly put his backpack down, sat at the table, and put his face in his hands. "I can't do anything right. I'm a complete loser," he whispered to his mom, almost as if he were speaking more to himself than to her.

His mom felt terrible. Statements like these are painful for any parent to hear. If my child feels like a failure, we say to ourselves, then I must have failed in some important way, too.

But rather than get busy trying to convince our children that they really aren't failures, we first have to sympathize with the feeling, then try to figure out whether this is merely a passing mood due to a bad report card or not catching a fly ball during after-school baseball practice or part of a bigger problem of low self-esteem or developing depression.

PARENT TIPS

- "Our son felt like a failure because he was lousy at every sport he tried. So we checked out the Saturday morning activities program at the local Y. When we visited the ceramics workshop, Kris wanted to sign up and found he loved the class. Now he brings the pots he's made to school, and when his friends start talking about sports, he reminds himself that he's good at something, too," says Paige, mother of 3.

Failure and self-esteem

What parents have to remember is that failing is not *necessarily* a terrible experience. After all, the ages from five to thirteen are full of challenges, and our kids can't always succeed the first time around with a new friend, a tennis serve, or long division. One important part of growing up is learning how to persevere despite mistakes, setbacks, and failure.

How your kids explain why they failed tells you a lot about their sense of confidence and self-esteem. Kids with high self-esteem bounce back fairly quickly. If they fail a test they may say, "Well, that test was pretty hard. I guess I didn't study enough." They assume effort and persistence count in mastering anything, so they make a plan to study more next time! Kids with low self-esteem may say "I guess I'm just stupid," and assume there's not much they can do to change things in the future.

Most children can identify whether a specific incident is at the root of their feelings or if they're reacting to a series of small incidents that have finally overwhelmed them. We can help our kids review what actually did happen, experts say, then plan small steps toward overcoming the obstacles they encountered, and make sure the challenges they've undertaken are realistic for their age and abilities so they *do* experience some success. Continual failure makes everyone discouraged.

Your child is probably concerned about failing in one of three areas: friendship, sports, or schoolwork.

"Nobody likes me!"

Being popular is an important goal for many kids, but according to psychologists, having one good friend is all they need to not feel as if they're social failures—at least until middle school. That's when they calibrate exactly where they fall in the class social hierarchy. They may feel like failures unless they can be part of the "top" group, as Sally did. Her mom helped her see that it was unrealistic to expect these girls to be her close friends because they were athletic whereas she wasn't interested in sports.

With a younger child, investigate. Look for explanations if he or she isn't being invited to parties or for playdates. Some children have trouble making and keeping friends and need some social skills coaching. Rita noticed that her daughter, who said no one wanted to play with her, interrupted her playmates and was very bossy. Rita told her daughter, "Let's practice some things that will make you a better friend."

"I stink at school!"

By the time children reach fourth and fifth grade, academic work intensifies and children who can't keep up begin to feel as if something's wrong with them, as in "I must just be dumb." To avoid this, keep abreast of what's going on at school so you can prevent serious problems from developing. A study routine at home helps kids feel more on top of their work—and lets you help them plan for school success. If you see a downward trend in grades, make an appointment to see the teacher. Your child may need extra help in a particular subject.

Kids with undiagnosed learning disabilities often feel like failures. So do unathletic kids, especially boys, unless they find a group with interests similar to their own.

Each child is unique

Sadly, parents—and teachers—contribute to feelings of failure by comparing kids and praising one more than another. If your daughter overhears you say to her brother, "Another perfect report card from the star student in our family," you can bet that she'll feel like a failure even if her report card is only slightly less stellar. Accepting our kids' individual strengths and weaknesses is another essential. A boy who is a fabulous drummer will still feel like a failure if his dad thinks sports are everything and expresses disappointment that his son is not a star on the hockey team. Children can carry that sense of failure into their adult lives, no matter how much they accomplish. ❑

DID YOU KNOW?

◆ Boys and girls differ significantly over issues of academic performance. According to a famous study by Carol Dweck, when boys are successful they credit themselves, but when they fail, they blame others, such as teachers; girls, on the other hand, credit others for their successes and blame themselves when they fail.

When Your Child Is Nervous & Anxious

"I have a bad feeling about today," nine-year-old Jimmy announces gloomily at breakfast. "I just know something bad is going to happen to me. I don't know what, but it will." Maybe his teacher snaps at the kids, and he's worried today is his turn. Maybe a classmate warned him that not everyone can play in the ball game at recess. Maybe he didn't do his math homework as thoroughly as he should have.

Like many parents of anxious kids, Jimmy's have been through many such mornings. No matter how they try to reassure their son, he still feels worked up. They can't pinpoint what's troubling him and haven't been able to help him calm down. As a result, they are becoming frustrated—and exasperated with Jimmy.

Teach calming techniques

Anxiety is a vicious cycle. The more preoccupied our kids are with how anxious and nervous they feel, the more anxious they get! That's why they need to learn a specific calming technique they can turn to as soon as they notice the telltale signs of anxiety—dizziness, racing pulse, quick, shallow breathing, and sometimes nausea.

First, focus on breathing. Even children as young as five or six years of age can learn to sit still, breathe in deeply through the nose, hold their breath, and then let out the breath slowly and evenly through the mouth. Just a few minutes of doing this soothes the racing nervous system and restores a measure of tranquility.

Second, teach kids to say a mantra. Repeating this simple phrase over and over to yourself is a technique that helps kids—and adults—to calm down. I found saying "Everything will turn out fine" reduced my anxiety even when I was stuck in traffic on the way to the airport. When my son Jake is anxious about a test, he invents a mantra of his own. One favorite is "I studied and I'm prepared."

Visualizing something fun, like jumping in a pile of leaves or into a swimming pool, can take kids' minds off worrying, too.

Of course, it's best to teach children these techniques when they *aren't* anxious!

"What's the worst-case scenario?"

Chronic worriers are always anticipating disaster. Once your child is calm, you can help him or her look at the future in a more realistic way. If Terri freezes up before a soccer game, for example, her mom, Leah, plays this game.

"What's the worst thing that could happen?" she asks.

"I could miss kicking a goal," Terri says.

"Then what would happen?"

"My teammates would be very disappointed in me."

"Then what?"

"They'd tell me, or they'd groan, or they'd say something."

ASK THE EXPERTS

- **According to New York City psychologist David Gottesfeld, children who are chronically anxious about school may have an underlying, undiagnosed learning or attention deficit disorder. These children need to be evaluated to identify any neurological causes for their anxiety.**

"Then what?"

"I'd tell them that I tried, and that everyone makes mistakes."

"Then what?"

"They'd agree with me."

This kind of open-ended "what if" questioning—which many elementary-school-age kids love—gradually reassures many of them that they can handle any situation that may arise.

Draw on past successes

Anxious kids also tend to underestimate their abilities to cope, so it helps to remind them of when and how they have. When Sam gets nervous about a test, his dad starts the "remember when" dialogue:

"Do you remember when you were nervous about last week's spelling test? What were you worried about?"

"That I'd forget everything."

"And what happened?"

"I studied and only got two wrong."

"What are you worried about now?"

"That I'll forget everything."

"What do you think will happen?"

"I'll study tonight. If I do, I may still forget some words, but not all of them."

Predictability and planning ahead

Worry thrives on unpredictability. So it's no surprise that kids who are anxious cope best when home and school routines are the same every single day—at least as much as possible. Not knowing what to expect is what makes new experiences so anxiety-provoking. Annie's big worry about attending a new school was that she wouldn't be able to find her classes. So her parents set up a tour of the building the week before school began. They also suggested she develop a "just in case" plan of what to do if she did get lost—to go in any class and ask how to find the office.

Nervousness frequently surfaces after an unexpected success like being selected for a special class or asked out on a date. Instead of paying attention to the present, kids start worrying about whether they'll ever succeed again, as Petra did after winning first place at the school science fair.

Petra's mom advised, "Worry about that next year. Right now, enjoy this moment." ❑

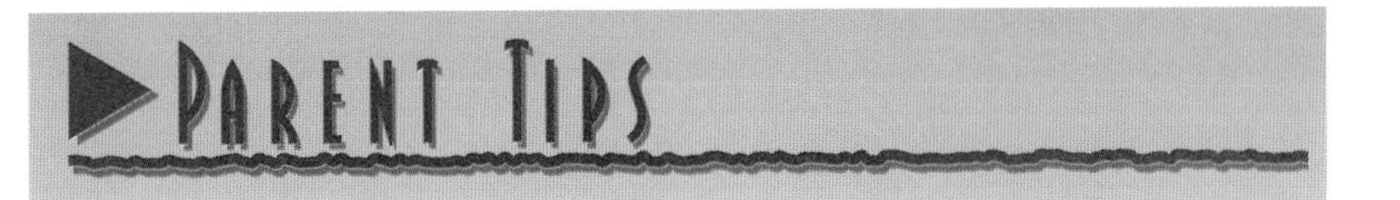

- "Eli gets very nervous before tests. I help him draw up a study plan—which pages to review, which sections to take notes on. Then I ask him whether he'll quiz himself on the material or have me quiz him. Once these details are worked out, his anxiety goes down," says his father, Frank.
- "Our daughter gets anxious during transitions—when she is going to a friend's house or starting day camp, for example. We called this pattern to her attention. Now we say, 'It's one of those times,' and Gayle reminds herself she's been in this situation before," says her mom, Molly.

About Fears

"The sky grew dark and the wind gusty, and my son Trevor was growing paler by the moment," remembers his mom, Antonia. "When he heard a loud crack of thunder and lightning flashed, he ran into his room, climbed into bed, and pulled the covers over his head. 'Make it stop!' he cried. I wish I could have. The storm raged for about thirty minutes, and Trevor was terrified the entire time."

Like Antonia, most of us wish we could prevent our kids' fears. But we're all born with two: a fear of falling and a fear of loud noises. Sometime in the first year of life we become afraid when we're separated from our caretakers. And that's just the beginning! Another year, another fear . . .

Our real job is to help kids identify what they're afraid of, figure out how to reassure them they're safe, and come up with ways they can conquer their fears.

Fearsome creatures

No fears are imaginary to a five- or six-year-old! Dinosaurs in the closet, a monster under the bed, and wild animals down the hall are all very real. Some kids also become inexplicably afraid of fictional characters from cartoons or the movies. When one of my sons was five he could watch the creepiest cartoon about robots, but something about Maria dressed up as the Little Tramp on *Sesame Street* scared him so much we had to shut off the TV and huddle together until he was sure the program was over.

For kids, burglars are fearsome creatures, too, and they *know* they're real.

Most parents quickly learn that what helps kids are night lights, open bedroom doors, closet doors closed tight—maybe with a latch—a flashlight on the floor by the side of a child's bed, a large stuffed animal in bed to act as a heroic, protective companion, and a baseball bat under the bed for "just in case." Think of these as props your children can use to feel powerful enough to withstand their fears.

Humor and stories help, too. My friend Charles told his son, "Did you know that monster you're afraid of is afraid of anyone who says the word 'Bupple'? Why don't we say it loud, together?"

Trevor's mother told him, "When we hear thunder, the Thunder Cloud family is playing a game called Thunder Ball. A loud thunderclap is like a home run." During the next thunderstorm, he kept score with his mom instead of being scared.

Give reassurance and a reality check

First, reassure kids they're safe. Though we've probably all said, "You have nothing to be afraid of," at one time or another, that *doesn't* reassure kids or help them get over a fear, even one that sounds infantile or unrealistic to you. Instead, say experts, it often makes them feel ashamed. But

AGE FACTOR

❖ Academically gifted children have fears that are typical of kids much older than they are, according to a study by University of Cincinnati psychologist Richard Klene. The fears of a gifted 8-year-old, for example, resembled those of a 12-year-old.

don't magnify a fear out of all proportion, either, by listing all the things to watch out for! Neither of these approaches builds a child's confidence.

Besides listening seriously to kids' fears, parents need to give children, especially young ones afraid of insects, animals, and nature in general, factual information they can balance against those fears. After all, young children don't know that loud thunder won't affect the house or that grizzly bears don't live in the woods down the road. Older children benefit from real information, too—they may not know that most of the kids in the eighth grade are just as scared as they are that no one will dance with them at the school party.

Expose kids gradually

Facing fears, researchers say, is the only way to get rid of them—whether a person is five or ten or thirteen or thirty. But we have to build our kids' ability to do this with small steps. Start slowly by exposing your child indirectly to what he or she fears. Dan's mom read him a book about spiders, and then they watched a video of *Charlotte's Web*. After Dan had become fascinated by how spiders spin webs and by the character of Charlotte the spider, Dan's mom moved on to to something more direct. She told him, "I'm going to look at some spiders on the porch. You watch me from the doorway. The spiders won't even notice me." When nothing happened, Dan was able to say bravely, "I'll come and see how big the spider is myself," and do it.

Separation fears

Some children's fears require other types of reassurance. When five- and six-year-olds are afraid of going to school or to sleep, seven- and eight-year-olds of getting lost in a huge store, and eight- and nine-year-olds about their parents becoming ill and dying, they're all in the throes of the same basic fear of separation.

To handle this, we have to be straightforward and truthful. Something *could* happen to you while your child is at school; it *is* possible to get lost in a store; parents *do* get sick. To pretend otherwise is dishonest. Instead, as experts advise, I make the distinction between "possible" and "probable," and offer specific advice. In a big store, that might mean showing a six-year-old the guard at the front of the store and saying, "If we get separated, we'll meet back here by the guard."

Unfortunately, there are no such guidelines to assuage a child's fear of death. Experts advise using events in the natural world as well as your own religious beliefs to explain death. Like many parents, I find it best to speak from my heart. "It would be scary and sad if I were to die," I tell my nine-year-old. "But I'm healthy and do the things that will help me live a long time."

ASK THE EXPERTS

Dr. Stephen W. Garber, author of *Monsters Under the Bed,* says the 4 most effective ways to quell a child's fears are:

- **Ask your child to imagine a scene in which she overcomes her fear.**
- **Give her reliable information from books.**
- **Expose her indirectly to things she fears, by having her observe others confronting them.**
- **Expose her directly, in small, gradual doses, to something she fears.**

ASK THE EXPERTS

- **"Children's fears come and go, but almost 90% of children develop certain fears appropriate for their age," writes psychologist Benjamin B. Wolman in his book *Children's Fears.* He says that fears of darkness, noise, and storms and fears of imaginary and supernatural dangers such as ghosts and goblins decline with age.**

Social fears

If you think back to your own childhood, you'll remember how fears about social acceptability abounded. When our kids have similar fears, they love to hear stories about how we went through the same trials and tribulations. They also like us to remind them of when they managed to conquer their fears and hear us retell their own success stories.

At the same time, look for specific ways to alleviate your child's fears. Mentally walking through what will happen at a social event in advance and pinpointing exactly what seems scary is sometimes enough to give kids confidence. Other kids feel calmer when they plan a role for themselves—arranging the food or bringing a stack of CDs to play. Peg, like many middle schoolers, was afraid of saying "something stupid" to the boy she liked at a class party. "He probably feels that way, too," her mom advised. Then she helped her daughter list a few questions to ask him.

Performance fears

Who hasn't had the nightmare of having to take a surprise test? Or of standing in front of a crowd to give a speech and having no voice? In fact, these are fears of performing and making a mistake. If your child is afraid of being called on in class or giving an oral report, stage some dress rehearsals at home in advance. Bill had his shy son practice reading aloud and taping it to get him used to the sound of his own voice. If your child seems unsure physically, karate and sports can increase confidence. It's also helpful for kids to know that being afraid doesn't mean they can't go on. Most actors are, and they do. We can feel afraid and still do well on a test. The goal isn't to banish fear, but to reduce its power.

Use "magic" charms

Remember the story of Dumbo, who thought the feather he carried enabled him to fly? We all feel more secure with a good luck charm in our pocket to remind us of home and give us courage. Trish took her favorite stuffed animal to school in her backpack so she could take it out or touch it when she felt homesick. Even older kids cherish objects like Dad's St. Christopher medal or Mom's special locket.

The best charms, however, are intangible. "Whenever you're afraid," my friend tells her children, "I want you to picture how safe you feel when I tuck you into bed each night." Other children evoke images of protective older siblings, grandparents, pets, or God to help them through fearful times.

Check what they watch

There are plenty of scary images in movies and TV shows, and as many parents discover at bedtime, these are often the source of a child's fears. Kids find many items on the nightly news scary, too, especially if some horror involves a child their own age. Check out what your children are watching and ask yourself if it's appropriate. We can prevent some fears by turning off the TV and avoiding certain movies, and reassure kids that what they see on the news is very unlikely to happen to them.

When is a fear a phobia?

While most childhood fears can be put to rest, phobias are fears so severe that they interfere with a child's functioning. Some involve objects that aren't necessarily scary, like escalators; others arise from an actual trauma. Jenny, for example, became afraid of all dogs after a German shepherd jumped on her and nipped her arm. Age matters, too. A six-year-old's fear of strangers is normal, but in a twelve-year-old the same fear is phobic.

Experts say indirect and then direct, gradual exposure to the feared object works best. That's the process we followed when my son developed a phobia of injections. While many kids are afraid of shots because they hurt, Jake's fear was extreme—he broke out in a sweat and started shaking and crying on the way to the doctor's office.

First Jake watched the doctor handle the needle. Then I held it, pointing out how tiny it was. Next, our sensitive pediatrician suggested that my son hold it, which he did, tentatively. When he still looked terrified, our doctor suggested he pick a day the following week to come back for the shot. In the intervening days, we read books about doctors and discussed how the shot would protect him from getting serious diseases.

With information and some control over his fate, Jake was able to overcome his phobia in a relatively short time. Other phobias may prove to be more resistant. In these cases, it's best to consult with your pediatrician. ❑

DID YOU KNOW?

- One of the most effective ways to make children less afraid is to have them watch a child their age deal confidently with a similar situation. A 6-year-old who is afraid of dogs, for example, will probably be less afraid after watching another 6-year-old play with the same dog.
- Children are most vulnerable to phobias between the ages of 3 and 6.

When Your Child Feels Shy Or Embarrassed

Alma, a sixth grader, was running for president of the student council. She spent a week writing her campaign speech, enlisting her dad's help every evening after dinner. When the big day came, she tripped while climbing the stairs to the stage in front of the entire student body. Near tears, she rushed through her speech, mumbling every word, sure that everyone was secretly laughing at her. That night she moaned, "It was awful, Dad. I can't go back to school. I was so embarrassed!"

Have you heard similar words from your child? Most parents of school-aged kids have, especially parents of self-conscious preteens. There's not too much we can do when our kids are embarrassed, except be aware of what embarrasses them, sympathize, tell a story of the time we dropped the cake the class had made for a teacher's going-away party, and remind them, as Alma's dad did, of their many strengths.

Being in the limelight

For most kids, being the center of attention makes them self-conscious, and they become embarrassed if they make a mistake. The moment Leona's mom asks her to perform a cartwheel for a friend who's visiting, the six-year-old stumbles and can't do one, and then gets embarrassed. But her embarrassment won't last long if her mom doesn't make a big deal out of it and reminds her of how well she performed an hour before. If Leona were ten, though, her embarrassment might linger. The moral: don't put preteens, who would rather not be noticed at all, on the spot.

Public praise can also evoke embarrassed feelings in preteens. In fact, the older kids are, the more they feel embarrassed when complimented publicly. If you like the way your twelve-year-old looks or are pleased by the report card he brings home, remember that many kids this age prefer being told matter-of-factly.

Parents are an embarrassment, too

Eleven- to thirteen-year-olds are often just as self-conscious about their parents as they are about themselves. As a result they suffer agonies of embarrassment over our very presence, not to mention our minor eccentricities, like wearing a pair of old blue shorts and humming when we drive their friends to a school party.

Before you get too irritated when they say, "Mom, you're embarrassing me," think back. You may remember a time when you wished your parents were invisible, too. Try to be understanding, keep your sense of humor, and if you can, indulge their requests.

The shyness factor

All kids get embarrassed at one time or another but not all are shy. Shyness is basically a matter of inborn temperament.

◆ Charles Darwin devoted the last chapter of his book *The Expression of the Emotions in Man and Animals* to shame and embarrassment. He claims that "blushing is the most peculiar and the most human of all expressions," the emotion that distinguishes us from all the other animals.

Dr. Jerome Kagan, who has studied it extensively, found that about twenty percent of kids are born shy and are more fearful than other children of strangers, changes, new situations, and being embarrassed. He also found that parents can help them be more outgoing.

Some children, however, don't turn shy until middle school. Then they begin feeling highly self-conscious about their appearance and performance and get extremely anxious in new social situations.

Overcoming shyness

Think of shyness as a behavior or habit that can be changed somewhat, but don't expect changes to happen quickly. A shy child probably won't grow up to be the life of the party, but with a loving mixture of challenge and help, he can turn into a self-confident teenager and adult.

Don't let kids off the hook. Don't overprotect shy kids, even preteens. Instead challenge them to take small steps in reaching out socially. Chuck was so shy that he didn't even want to invite classmates over for a birthday party. Rather than indulge his wish, his mom suggested that he invite just one friend over to watch a video and have birthday cake. Then she set up some incentives to encourage him to have one friend over to play each week.

Teach and practice social skills. Shy children sometimes need help learning social skills, like how to say hello, play common games, act friendly and smile, and read others' moods (see page 80-81).

They also need more preparation and advance practice for social situations than other kids do. If your son is afraid of attending his first Little League practice, take him to the field when no one is there, as Don did with his son, Nick, so he could accustom himself to the setting. They also rehearsed what Nick could say when he first met his teammates. Before every junior high party, Margo's dad reminds her, "When you feel shy, stop and look around. If you see someone standing alone, assume they're shy too, and go over and say hello."

Many shy adults say that the most difficult part of being a shy child was the fact that their parents ignored their shyness instead of helping them

Build self-confidence. Often being part of an organized group led by an adult helps shy kids to become more confident. Timid Ellen felt comfortable in Brownies, where the troop leader often paired Ellen with another shy girl in activities. Since Ellen also loved to draw, her mom enrolled her in a small art class where her talent was admired by other kids. Being involved in a team sport or some other after-school activity is very helpful to shy preteens.

What else helps? Remind your child—and praise her—for the times she overcame her shyness. ❑

ASK THE EXPERTS

According to psychologist Jonathan M. Cheek:

- **Thirty to 40% of school-aged children and adults say they are shy.**
- **Shyness peaks during 7th and 8th grades, when 60% of girls and 48% of boys call themselves shy.**
- **Less than 50% of those children who became shy as adolescents still feel shy by age 21.**

When Your Child Feels Guilty Or Ashamed

When you think about it, shame and guilt have both a positive side and a negative side. Too much of these feelings can prove crippling and often lead to depression in kids.

But children who never experience guilt or shame also have problems. These emotions alert us to the fact that we didn't behave as well as we should have and urge us to do better in the future.

So our goal as parents isn't to protect our children from all experiences of guilt and shame, but instead to help them use these feelings to motivate themselves to become better people.

What's the difference between shame and guilt?

Shame appears when children first develop the ability to evaluate themselves. If kids fail at tasks they believe they should be able to do, they feel ashamed. Many middle-school boys who are being bullied, for example, are very ashamed that they haven't been able to stop the bullying. That's why they so often keep what's happening a secret. But children may also feel ashamed of any number of things about themselves—being short, having a braying laugh, or because their parents wear odd clothes. Shame results not from a situation, but from how kids think about it.

When kids feel ashamed, they condemn themselves in a global way, as in "I'm a terrible person," and usually they believe this is something that they can't change.

Guilt, on the other hand, is a specific reaction to a specific situation. When kids feel guilty, they focus on actions, not themselves, and are aware there is something they can do to fix the situation.

How parents contribute

Sadly, when we blame our kids for things over which they have no real control, like having angry thoughts or feelings, or hold them to unrealistically high standards they can't meet, they often react by feeling deeply ashamed. And when we use guilt tactics to make them behave, as in "You wouldn't wear baggy jeans if you loved me," kids eventually turn angry, vengeful, and rebellious.

Overcoming shame

If we don't show kids ways to overcome shame, they're liable to carry it a long time, as I did. When I was in the fifth grade, my good friend Janice and I were threatened by three tough older boys as we walked home. We started to run, but I soon streaked ahead. Although I looked back and saw the boys gaining on her, did I turn back to help her? Not on your life. I ran all the way home, and I knew that I was behaving despicably.

Over time, my shame increased. How could I have deserted my friend like that? I couldn't tell anyone for years.

What helps kids—and would have helped me—stop thinking they're "awful"? Shame often abates when we tell the story. Confessing to my mom would have been a good first step, along with talking to Janice. Giving kids a private diary in which they can record their feelings works wonders, but we can also let them know we're available and won't condemn them when they want to unburden themselves.

Put guilt to work

Guilt is easier to alleviate than shame, and parents can encourage kids to find ways to make amends for something they did wrong, as Adrienne's mom did.

Twelve-year-old Adrienne overheard a girl in her class talking about a CD she was eager to buy after school—it was the only copy left in the store. Adrienne wanted that CD, too, and she hurried to the store after school and bought it.

Later, she felt very guilty. "I shouldn't have done that," she moaned to her mom. "It was so selfish. What should I do?"

Adrienne's mom agreed that what she had done wasn't very nice and brainstormed with her, asking her what would make *her* feel better if the situation were reversed. She was pleased—and said so—when Adrienne decided to call her classmate, explain what happened, apologize, and offer the girl the CD.

Adrienne doesn't worry that she's an awful person; she understands that her *actions* were wrong and by rectifying them feels good about herself.

The more we help kids learn to evaluate their actions rather than their entire being, the less shameful and the more in control of themselves they will be. ❑

ASK THE EXPERTS

- **In a study of 200 students, psychologist Michael Lewis found that girls are 3 times more likely than boys to be ashamed if they fail at performing an easy task.**

Teach Kids To Be Happy, Hopeful, & Optimistic

My grandmother had an enormous lap—large enough to gather all five of her grandchildren together, and squeeze us tight. "Just be happy, children," she'd say to us with such intensity that I almost believed she could make it happen.

As parents we're all too aware that wishing won't make our kids happy or hopeful about life. Of course, we know they can't be happy all the time. There are plenty of situations that demand other emotions, like anger or sadness. What most of us mean when we say we want our children to be happy is that we want them to have the self-confidence to take risks, meet challenges, achieve their goals, feel good about themselves, and greet at least some days with joy. How can we encourage this?

Teach optimism

Whether our kids see a glass as half-empty or half-full depends in part on their temperament. But according to psychologist Martin Seligman, author of *The Optimistic Child*, children who are pessimistic also think about events in a way that makes them feel as if they are at fault and have no control over what happens. Optimistic kids, on the other hand, assume that they'll be able to overcome the obstacles they encounter—a friend got mad at them today but they can apologize and make up, they got a C on an exam but can study harder next time. Parents, says Seligman, can help pessimistic kids learn to be more optimistic. Here's how:

Catch negative thoughts. Nine-year-old Joanne came home from an afternoon at a friend's house and told her mom, "Denise doesn't like me any more. I'm a terrible friend." When her mother asked what happened, Joanne explained that Denise suddenly said she didn't want to play and went upstairs to turn on the TV. Because of this, Joanne decided that she was a bad friend. If she catches this negative thought, though, she can reconsider it.

Reevaluate what you think. Joanne's mom asked questions to help her daughter think about the situation in a more objective way: "How long have you and Denise been friends?" "How often do you play with her?" "Why do you think she likes you to come over?" These made Joanne think about the positive and happy parts of the friendship and realize she's not a bad friend, after all.

Look for additional explanations. Next, Joanne's mom asked, "Could there be another reason why Denise went up to her room to watch TV besides not liking you any more?" Joanne realized that there might be many reasons—perhaps Denise was tired, she wasn't feeling well, or there was a program she wanted to watch.

Decide what to do next time. Joanne liked playing with Denise but admitted Denise could be moody. "If she does that

ASK THE EXPERTS

• Dr. Shelley E. Taylor's work shows that "positive illusions" often accompany optimism. People who think about themselves in slightly self-aggrandizing ways, are overly confident about their ability to control events around them, and are occasionally unrealistically optimistic about the future tend to have good mental health.

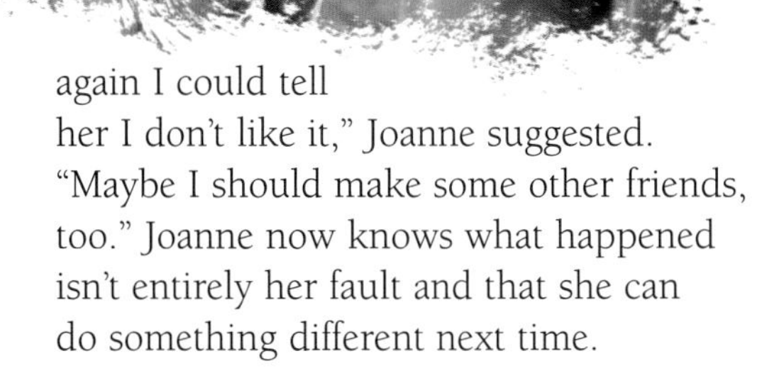

again I could tell her I don't like it," Joanne suggested. "Maybe I should make some other friends, too." Joanne now knows what happened isn't entirely her fault and that she can do something different next time.

Reinforce good feelings

In our time-pressed lives, we sometimes forget to make room for laughter and good moments with our kids every day. Reviewing the good things that happened during the day at bedtime and doing fun things together, such as watching a hilarious movie, are two ways we help kids focus on the positive in their lives. Abby, mother of two, consciously tries to reinforce good feelings by saying often: "That was fun, wasn't it?" "You must feel really great to have done that!" "Wow, I bet that made you happy."

Instill hope for the future

All of us meet with adversity in the real world at some time. Children who have hope, however, don't assume that barriers to happiness or fulfillment are inevitable or permanent. The way we instill this kind of hopefulness in kids is by being honest with them and showing them that we are optimistic about their abilities to make things happen differently in the future. When Franklin came home with a so-so report card, his dad said, "You didn't devote enough time to school this semester, and that neglect shows in your grades. I know you can do better."

Franklin stormed out of the kitchen. But later he said, "I thought about what you said, Dad. I didn't work as hard as I could have. I'll do better next semester."

When parents set such a cycle of hopefulness in motion, children tend to wake up each morning thinking that there's always a next time, another chance, the possibility of a new beginning. ❑

- "I feel happy when my family takes a trip together to the beach or an amusement park," says Tammie, 6.
- "I feel happy when my older brother agrees to play a game with me and lets me win sometimes," says Charles, 10.
- "What makes me cheerful? A weekend when I don't have a lot of homework and I can sleep late and my parents don't bug me about cleaning my room and I can just hang out with my friends," says Liam, 13.

Teach Kids To Read Others' Moods & Emotions

As we're learning to read our children's moods and emotions, they're learning to read ours, too. Sometimes they surprise us with how accurate they are. Jake and I were in the kitchen one afternoon when Ben returned from school. "Watch what you say to Mom," Jake told his older brother. "She's pretty grumpy today."

I thought I'd done a very good job of disguising my bad mood, so I asked Jake how he knew. "Easy," he said, "from the way you sighed when I asked you for another glass of milk."

Zeroing in on their parents' moods is the first step kids take toward understanding how other people feel and being able to see things from someone else's point of view—in other words, toward developing empathy. It's easy to see why kids who can make sense out of other people's actions, posture, and tone of voice usually get along better with their parents, other children, and even teachers. It also turns out that they do better in school. Sadly, the kids who don't learn these things often have a hard time making friends and can end up socially isolated.

These are powerful reasons to help your children learn the essentials of reading others' moods and emotions.

The basics of people reading

If your children are young, teach them to associate facial expressions and body language with certain feelings. Jody does this regularly with her five-year-old daughter, Sonya. When she surprised Jody one Saturday morning by coming down to breakfast entirely dressed, for example, Jody exaggerated her reaction—she opened her eyes very wide, dropped her mouth open, and said, "I'm so surprised!"

To help her sons understand how tone of voice conveys mood, one of my friends plays this game: each of them takes a statement—"What a beautiful picture!"—and says it in many different tones, exaggerating each, first honestly, then enviously, then sarcastically.

Try people watching

If you have older kids, try to catch them in various moods and point out their body language, tone, and expressions. If your son feels angry after his soccer team loses a match, you might say, "Those fists look as if they want to pound something into

- "My daughter and I look through the newspaper and magazines together to find provocative pictures of people. We pretend they're characters in a comic strip, draw balloons above their heads, and write in what we think they might be saying," says Molly, mother of a 10-year-old.

pieces." Use yourself as an example, too, as in "When I get very quiet and purse my lips like this, it means I'm getting mad."

The Morris family likes to watch TV with the sound off and come up with their own explanations of how the characters are feeling and what they're saying based on body language and facial expressions.

And when my kids and I find ourselves sitting in the car in a traffic jam or outside a store, we entertain ourselves by people watching and try to figure out what their conversations are about or what they're thinking to themselves.

Gentle reminders

Even kids who are the most astute readers of others' feelings sometimes get carried away and, in the heat of the moment, don't pick up on the signs others give. Ten-year-old Melanie tends to get a little manic when a friend is over. Her mom has noticed that she starts talking a mile a minute and that eventually her friend's eyes glaze over and she retreats, as if she's overwhelmed.

Melanie and her mom ultimately agreed on a signal. When her mom says quietly, "Chill, Melanie," she remembers that she's supposed to stop whatever she's doing and look at her friend. If her friend doesn't look interested, then Melanie says, "Hey, what would you like to do?"

In the family

Living together in close quarters, most families come to know each others' emotional habits pretty well.

If Jolie doesn't play the radio while she's getting dressed in the morning, her dad knows she's in a bad mood. Barbara knows that her younger son is troubled by something from the way he says good night. If he turns over right away, she says, he's fine. If he hesitates, Barbara knows he's worried about something and wants to talk.

We can call these signs to our kids' attention, too, by saying something like "Your sister's not talking on the phone tonight. That usually means she's upset about something. What do you think?" Even a six-year-old might be sensitive enough to respond, "I guess I should leave her alone." ❑

ASK THE EXPERTS

• Psychologist Carolyn Saarni of Sonoma State University in California observes, "Children who can accurately read others' emotions are generally the most socially competent children in their peer group."

Ways To Improve Your Home's Emotional Climate

Every family is different, with different personalities, customs, and ways of thinking, talking, and connecting to one another. There is no one "right" kind of family. But whether parents are strict or lenient, boisterous or calm, home has to be a place of love, encouragement, and acceptance of their feelings and individuality for kids to feel emotionally safe and secure. It also has to be a source of don'ts and limits.

Most of us want such an atmosphere to prevail in our homes, but with today's stresses this often seems harder and harder to achieve. From time to time it helps to take stock and think about the changes we could make to improve our home's emotional climate. Here are a few that will.

Watch what you say

How we talk to our children every day is part of the emotional atmosphere we weave. Besides giving them opportunities to be open about how they feel, we have to watch what we say and how we say it.

We often forget how much kids take parental criticisms to heart and how much these affect their feelings about themselves. Psychologist Martin Seligman found that when parents consistently blame kids in exaggerated ways, children feel overly guilty and ashamed and withdraw emotionally. Look at the difference between "Roger, this room is always a pigsty! You are such a slob!" and "Roger, your room is a mess today! Before you go out to play, it has to be picked up."

One way tells Roger he can never do anything right. The other tells him exactly what to do to fix things so he can be back in his mom's good graces and doesn't suggest he has a permanent character flaw. For criticism to be constructive for children, we have to cite causes that are specific and temporary.

Another constructive way to criticize children is to remind them of the impact their actions have on us. This promotes empathy rather than resentment.

Provide order and stability

A predictable daily framework, clear and consistent rules, and an organized house make kids—and parents—more relaxed and comfortable, and that means everyone has emotional equilibrium. When conflicts, tensions, or crises occur, the routine is a reassuring and familiar support, a reliable strand of our lives that won't change.

Think about *your* mornings. Do your kids go off to school feeling calm and confident? Or are they upset and grumpy?

What about evenings and bedtime? Do you have angry fights over homework or how much TV children can watch? A calm bedtime routine is one good antidote for the dark fears that surface when kids are alone in bed with the lights turned out.

Yet a routine that's too inflexible doesn't make room for kids' individual temperaments, preferences, and quirks.

Hold family meetings

Time together is at such a premium in most households that many families, like the Martins, hold regular family meetings so everyone can air and resolve the week's grievances as well as share the good things that happened.

When the Martins gather on Friday night, they also take the opportunity to anticipate what's scheduled for the week ahead. That way they eliminate (mostly!) those last minute anxieties over whether someone has soccer shoes for the first practice, the books for a report, or a ride to a music lesson.

Encourage loving feelings

Everyday life is full of opportunities to establish loving connections with our kids. Researchers have found that parents who spend time playing, joking with, and sharing their own thoughts and feelings with their kids have children who are more friendly, generous, and loving.

After all, giving love fosters love, and what convinces our kids that we love them more than our willingness to spend time with them? Many parents say that often they feel most in tune emotionally with their kids when they just hang out together—sprawling on the bed to watch TV, walking down the block together to mail a letter, talking on long car rides when kids know they have a parent's complete attention. At these times the hurt feelings and the secret fears are finally mentioned.

Part of encouraging loving feelings is insisting that kids treat others, including siblings, with kindness, respect, and fairness—at least some of the time. In one family, kids write on a chart in the kitchen at the end of each day the name of someone who did something nice for them.

- "My parents have something called the "Ask Once" rule. They tell me that I can ask them for anything—no matter how outrageous. But I can only ask once, and I have to take no for an answer. I like this rule, because I don't have to keep my thoughts to myself," says Richard, 10.

▶ Parent Tips

How do you create a good emotional atmosphere at home?

- "I don't shy away from talking about my own feelings. When I'm angry or sad or worried, I tell my kids, and explain why. And then I talk about how I'm handling these feelings," reports Patrick, father of a boy and a girl.
- "I keep a magnetic slate on the refrigerator and draw 5 faces on it. Each morning, when everyone in the family comes down for breakfast, we fill in a face that reflects how we feel—happy, grumpy, tired, worried, upset. And then we update our faces after we eat dinner," offers Marguerite, mother of 3 boys.
- "I try to plan one activity with my kids each day. Sometimes we go to the library; sometimes we water the plants. And if something on my daily agenda doesn't get done, that's okay," says Jill, mother of 2 girls.

Create rituals

Setting aside special times of the day or week to come together as a family gives children a sense of continuity—that certain feelings stay the same even as the kids change and grow. For many families, like my friend Frances', that means regularly observing religious rituals. To her family, Sunday morning means going to Mass and having hot chocolate afterwards at the town café. Others create their own rituals to anchor the week. Michael's family celebrates with a regular Scrabble and pizza party every Friday night; Dawn's goes to the movies. Holiday rituals give children points in the year to look forward to.

When challenges arise

Home life today is not always stable and secure. Even the best marriages have fights, economic woes, emotional ups-and-downs. Parents divorce, stepfamilies form, and these changes challenge the most compassionate parents. But troubles are part of the human condition. Loving families don't ignore them—they try to create a strong emotional climate despite them.

In handling parental conflicts, for example, we can let kids know when everything has been resolved, as Denise and Peter did after a loud dispute in the kitchen during which voices were raised and tears flowed. After making up, they explained to their kids, "Sometimes we disagree and lose our tempers, too. But now we've worked it out. We're sorry that you overheard our fight."

Schedule in parent-only time

Parents are the ones who create a home's atmosphere. When we're upset about how much money we owe, worried about downsizing at the company where we work, or angry at a spouse, that charges the emotional atmosphere in ways kids find threatening. As one friend said plaintively, "Parents need special time, too." Taking a long walk together to talk without our kids may go a long way to soothe worries and regular "parent-only" dates help us reexperience the love that brought us together in the first place. ❑

Does Your Child Need Professional Help?

Most problems our kids have with emotions and moods are common and temporary. All kids go through periods when they mope about, don't feel like eating, cry and play sad music on their CD player, are very anxious about a test, are angry with everyone, or make critical comments about themselves, as in "I stink at everything." Occasional bouts of any of these behaviors don't add up to a serious problem. Usually, we can help our children through these tough times by listening with empathy, taking their concerns seriously, coaching, and making changes at home. But not always.

How bad is it?

Some parents become alarmed at the first sign that their child may be having emotional trouble; other families are slow to pick up on signals of distress. As a general rule, assume that if your child's problems continue unabated for several weeks or more, your worries make sense.

Serious emotional problems also disrupt the normal flow of daily life and may start interfering with your child's activities. Tony, for example, doesn't go on sleepovers anymore because he wakes up screaming from nightmares every night. Other kids may have trouble sleeping or eating or may start acting the way they did at a much younger age.

What about your child's social life? He doesn't have to be popular to be emotionally healthy, but he should have at least one or two friends. If he's rarely invited on playdates or to parties and seems upset about it, then he may be having social difficulties.

Look for patterns

Children who are having emotional problems often seem locked into a pattern of behavior. When you talk with them, you begin to feel as if you're following a script. Every time you ask your daughter to do something like clean her room, for example, she responds by screaming, "You always criticize me. I can't take it any more!" At this point, you chime in with your predictable reply. This is a sign that you need help getting out of the rut.

Trust your feelings

You're the person who knows your child best. Use your instinctive feelings about him or her as a barometer—and be honest with yourself. Are you reluctant for your seven-year-old to invite a friend over because he often hits other kids or breaks their toys? Are you afraid of leaving your thirteen-year-old alone in the house, even for a short time, because you have reason to think he might hurt himself or do something rash? Do you dread conversations because your child usually turns them into an ugly scene? Of course, it's not always pleasant living with any preteen, but these are generally signs that your child needs outside help.

Listen to others

Ask other adults in your child's life to give you some feedback about your child. If a teacher, coach, or the parent of your child's friend is concerned about your child's well-being, take it seriously. They may be seeing something that you are missing.

What kind of help?

Start with your pediatrician. A surprising number of emotional problems are actually triggered by undetected medical problems. A child who seems depressed may actually have low blood sugar or an allergy. Even learning disabilities can masquerade as depression. All experts advise ruling out physical problems first.

If the problem is emotional, your pediatrician can probably recommend a psychologist or psychiatrist who has special training and experience working with children. You might also want to call your child's school and ask to speak to the psychologist. In fact, when problems involve social difficulties, the guidance counselor may be your best bet.

Asking for outside help is a hard step for many families to take. It's a little easier when you remind yourself that the sooner a problem is diagnosed and addressed, the more quickly it will be resolved. Most treatments are short-term, and the younger the child, the more flexible and open to treatment he or she usually is. ❑

YEAR BY YEAR

What To Expect At Different Ages

What To Expect At Different Ages—Kids' Feelings & Behavior

Many of our most basic emotions are actually present at birth, and the rest emerge by about age three. The situations and events that trigger feelings of happiness, anger, fear, frustration, and jealousy don't change much over time.

What changes with age. As children mature, however, the ways they interpret situations and understand, control, and express their feelings change. So does their ability to use emotional experiences to learn more about themselves and others. One reason is that children become more emotionally sophisticated as their cognitive abilities and language skills develop. As they grow, they also have more experiences with other kids, and these help them become aware of how their own moods and emotions have an impact on others.

Though there's no single blueprint to the process of becoming "emotionally intelligent," there are some general stages that most experts agree upon. Think of these as a continuum rather than a smooth upward progression with clear age markers. One seven-year-old may handle anger better than a nine-year-old; another may still express this emotion like a five-year-old.

Ages 5 to 7

- ***The importance of home***. Even though many children today attend preschool or daycare, most kindergartners are still very attached to their parents for guidance and support when they begin school. Shy children in particular may have some difficulty adjusting to the school environment, as do children who are very assertive and used to getting their way. By the age of seven kids are usually ready to come to school and do work without missing home.

  At home, some children experience intense sibling rivalry and jealousy toward one parent or the other.

- ***Fears of the unknown and known.*** Up until the age of six or so, most children are still trying to sort out the difference between fantasy and reality. They are often haunted by lingering fears of monsters, animals, darkness, and ghosts. At five, most kids' anxieties are still rooted in fear of separation from parents or caretakers, and phobias related to separation or the unknown sometimes surface.

  Wild animals, going to the doctor, getting a shot, the dark, new situations, and being alone are the common fears of first and sometimes second graders, and you're liable to see the first traces of performance anxiety. Many kids believe that more is being asked of them in school than they can handle. That often results in irritability and defiance.

- ***Making friends.*** Children begin to want to spend more time with their friends. At school and at home, they're often in situations with less adult supervision than they're used to, so many disputes arise.

The result is often anger. Kids are just beginning to learn that they can use words to modify how they're feeling.

• ***Coming to terms with limitations.*** Children often feel overwhelmed because their physical and cognitive skills are not developing as quickly as they wish. As a result, they often feel frustrated, and may even erupt in temper tantrums. Though tantrums aren't as frequent as they were a few years ago, five- and sometimes six-year-olds still have them, and they're usually caused by frustration. Being asked to hurry up, follow rules, and think of others before themselves can spark anger.

Ages 7 to 10

• ***Moving beyond the family***. Friends are increasingly important, and so are teachers, coaches, even parents of friends. Seven-year-olds are beginning to understand there are different types of love. Friendships are now based more on mutual interest. Jealousy and rivalry can be very intense as kids try to balance the conflicting emotional demands of these relationships. Disputes over rules and fairness, common at ages seven, eight, and nine, often end in anger.

• ***The need for constancy.*** Kids crave routine and are slow to adapt to change. Sometimes fears of new situations take over. Previously adventurous children may become more timid as they feel the world is less secure. As their conceptual understanding grows, children understand more with each year that death is final. Sadness takes on a new urgency. The death of grandparents or of pets, or the loss of a friend, looms very large. Kids may withdraw to regain emotional equilibrium and need time and loving attention to move beyond loss to new possibilities.

• ***Expanding horizons***. Children are gaining more competence in the world and a greater ability to control their emotions. Many now have a huge appetite for new experiences—they want to try every sport and after-school activity—and need help setting limits and planning realistic goals so they don't feel overwhelmed. They frequently complain about not having enough "down" time to restore themselves. Sufficient time for play and the freedom to loll around helps them consolidate what they feel.

• ***"How am I doing?"*** Because academic demands increase during third and fourth grades, many children become more anxious about grades and schoolwork. Fears of performing can arise. Kids frequently procrastinate and complain and grump about having too much work. They also begin to fear punishment.

• ***"I want to do it myself!"*** Kids' anger is often directed inward because children aren't as capable as they wish they were. They may feel especially encroached upon

AGE FACTOR

❖ According to a 1985 study, 83% of mothers and 64% of fathers were physically affectionate with their 5th graders. However, by the time the children were in 9th grade, only 48% of mothers and 33% of fathers said that they were physically affectionate.

by younger siblings, and grow increasingly possessive. Even when they're not angry or frustrated, younger ones can be whiny.

Having to make choices frustrates and angers children who feel tantalized by everything they see. They resent adults who try to assert control over them. Asking for their opinions and encouraging their participation in making decisions help quell their frustration and irritability.

Ages 10 to 13

- ***Moody middle schoolers***. Rapturous one moment, despondent the next—young preteens change their moods so fast it's hard for parents to keep up. This is related to hormonal changes and is more typical of eleven- and twelve-year-olds than thirteen-year-olds. Kids also start to become hypersensitive to perceived slights and moody and defiant, especially around parents. They frequently talk back and test the limits of acceptable behavior. Although they act as if they'd like parents to disappear, kids still need parents and are looking for ways to balance their needs for independence and dependence.
- ***The emerging peer group***. Younger kids on the cusp of puberty are caught up in the transition from elementary to middle school. Friends are beginning to eclipse parents in terms of importance—yet friendships can be mercurial and subject to change on an almost daily basis, leading to many hurt feelings, especially with girls. Kids are trying to figure out who they are and exactly where they fit in. Their insecurity about their social standing often surfaces as fearfulness, jealousy, or general moodiness. Some children become shy.
- ***Being different***. Not fitting in with the group is anathema to preteens. They fear standing out in any way. Everything—wearing the wrong hair clip, stumbling, laughing too loud—can prove mortifying and embarrassing.
- ***New fears and worries.*** Middle schoolers are very vulnerable to feelings of shame and embarrassment, mostly over their changing bodies and their newfound interest in the opposite sex. They also feel humiliated when they can't control their feelings. Worry about doing well in school and meeting their parents' expectations is another hallmark. The idea of growing up and being a teenager may seem scary to them at times. They are also susceptible to more adult fears—of failure, crowds, heights, and open spaces.
- ***"Don't treat me like a baby!"*** Many fights erupt at home, usually over such issues as limits and curfews. Kids act as if they wish they had no limits—though of course they not only need but want structure. What especially angers them is feeling shut out of the decision-making process. They like to have input regarding curfews and other rules governing their activities. ❑

WE RECOMMEND

Books, Games, Cassette Tapes, & Videos

BOOKS

For Kids in Elementary School

The following three series, favorites of five- to seven-year-olds, touch on feelings like affection, jealousy, fear, anger, and more:

THE BERENSTAIN BEARS
by Stan & Jan Berenstain (Random House)

Brother and Sister Bear learn about life from wise Mama Bear—and often Papa Bear learns with them.

FROG AND TOAD
by Arnold Lobel (HarperCollins)

Frog and Toad's touching, resilient friendship is the heart of the series.

LITTLE BEAR
by Else Holmelund Minarik (HarperTrophy)

Mama Bear and Baby Bear explore the emotional landscape of family life.

• • •

FEELINGS
by Aliki (Mulberry, 1984)

Children love Aliki's distinctive drawings and hand lettering. In this picture book, each page contains scenarios of how we react emotionally to different situations.

TALES OF A FOURTH GRADE NOTHING
by Judy Blume (Bantam Doubleday Dell, 1972)

Having two-year-old Fudge as a younger brother makes Peter feel his life is going nowhere. This old favorite for ages eight and up follows Peter as he sorts out his place in his family.

THE CHOCOLATE-COVERED-COOKIE TANTRUM
by Deborah Blumenthal (Clarion Books, 1996)

Sophie has a temper tantrum in the park when she sees a girl eating a delicious-looking cookie, but soon learns that there are better ways to get what she wants. A lovely picture book.

AMBER BROWN GOES FOURTH
by Paula Danziger (Scholastic, 1994)

Fourth-grade Amber wants to find a special friend this year, but it proves more difficult than she thought. Another winner in this series for kids ages eight and up.

GLAD MONSTER, SAD MONSTER:
A Book About Feelings
by Ed Emberley & Anne Miranda
(Little, Brown, 1997)

Five- and six-year-olds will love hearing about how monsters feel and then being asked how they feel. Each page is a mask kids can hold up to their faces to express a particular mood.

THE BEST WORST DAY
by Bonnie Graves (Hyperion, 1996)

The delights and difficulties of a best friend are detailed in this appealing chapter book for ages seven to nine.

BILLY, THE GHOST AND ME
by Gery Greer & Bob Ruddick
(HarperTrophy, 1997)

An I Can Read book for kids in grades two through four in the comic tall-tale tradition about what happens when two friends confront their worst fears and meet up with bank robbers.

Wilson Sat Alone
by Debra Hess (Simon & Schuster, 1994)

Wilson is a loner who does everything by himself until a new girl enters his class who's as shy as he is.

Class Clown
by Johanna Hurwitz (Scholastic, 1987)

Lucas experiments with becoming a new person in the third grade, but finds it harder than he thinks in this chapter book.

Mama, Do You Love Me?
by Barbara M. Joosse (Chronicle, 1991)

A tale of maternal love set in the Arctic, in which a young girl tests her mother's love by asking questions for which she receives honest answers. For five- and six-year-olds.

I Like Being Me:
Poems for Children, About Feeling Special, Appreciating Others, and Getting Along
by Judy Lalli and Douglas L. Mason-Fry (Free Spirit Publications, 1997)

This delightful anthology of poems and photos for ages five to eight covers feelings from unusual perspectives.

Alligator Baby
by Robert Munsch (Scholastic, 1997)

With eye-grabbing illustrations, this picture book chronicles fears and fantasies of first-borns over the arrival of a new baby.

No More Monsters for Me!
by Peggy Parish (HarperTrophy, 1981)

Imaginary monsters turn out to be harmless kittens in this I Can Read book.

Alexander and the Terrible, Horrible, No Good Very Bad Day
by Judith Viorst (Aladdin, 1987)

Alexander can't do anything right, and he gets into big trouble with his family at every turn in this wonderful picture book.

For Kids in Middle School

Are You There, God? It's Me, Margaret
by Judy Blume (Bantam Doubleday Dell, 1970)

A lonely, confused twelve-year-old girl strikes up conversations with God to see her through her hard times.

Seven Days To A Brand-New Me
by Ellen Conford (Scholastic, 1990)

Wallflower Maddy wants handsome Adam to notice her, so she buys a self-help manual that promises fast results. Adam's reaction is one she didn't anticipate.

The Private Notebook of Katie Roberts, Age 11
by Amy Hest (Candlewick Press, 1995)

Katie was only seven when her dad died during World War II, and four years later her mom remarries and moves from New York City to Texas, where Katie struggles to make a new life for herself, while still remembering her old one.

Your Move, J.P.!
by Lois Lowry (Dell, 1991)

Twelve-year-old J.P. suddenly starts acting very strange. What could be the explanation? It must be love!

Alice the Brave
by Phyllis Reynolds Naylor (Aladdin, 1995)
In the course of one summer, Alice learns to overcome the shame she feels over her water phobia, taking risks and finding inner courage.

Jacob I Have Loved
by Katherine Paterson (HarperTrophy, 1990)
This prize-winning story tells how twin sisters, different in every way, learn to work through their jealousy. It takes place on an island in Chesapeake Bay.

The War with Grandpa
by Robert Kimmel Smith (Dell, 1996)
This award-winning book explores a boy's anger and frustration with his grandfather, who moves in and changes life around the house in unexpected ways.

Dear Mom, You're Ruining My Life
by Jean Van Leeuwen (Puffin, 1990)
Samantha, who's much too tall, constantly gets into fights with her ever-embarrassing mother, but together they learn to negotiate the middle-school years.

For Parents

Know Your Child:
An Authoritative Guide for Today's Parents
by Stella Chess, M.D. and Alexander Thomas, M.D. (Jason Aronson, 1996)
This definitive book on temperament describes temperamental differences and stresses the importance of the fit between parents and their children.

Siblings Without Rivalry
by Adele Faber & Elaine Mazlish (Avon, 1987)
Jealousy is one of the many issues dealt with in this helpful book based on real problems from the authors' workshops.

The Roller Coaster Years:
Raising Your Child Through the Maddening Yet Magical Middle School Years
by Charlene C. Giannetti & Margaret Sagarese (Bantam Doubleday Dell, 1997)
This is one of the first books to focus on the "tween" years, when children are in middle school. It covers the hot topics for this age group: peer pressure, school, changing emotions, and much more.

Emotional Intelligence:
Why It Can Matter More than IQ
by Daniel Goleman (Bantam Books, 1995)
In his best-selling book, Goleman consolidates the research on emotional intelligence and competency, combining findings with true-to-life anecdotes.

The Heart of Parenting:
Raising An Emotionally Intelligent Child
by John Gottman, Ph.D. (Simon & Schuster, 1997)
A companion book to Goleman's, this one outlines the steps for parents to become emotional coaches for their kids. It includes dialogue, quizzes, and advice.

Playground Politics: Understanding the Emotional Life of Your School-Aged Child
by Stanley I. Greenspan, M.D. (Addison-Wesley, 1993)
Covering children ages five to twelve, this road map for parents discusses the

emotional rites of passage kids encounter in childhood. Greenspan discusses popularity, rivalry, rejection, and the social pecking order of the playground.

RAISING YOUR SPIRITED CHILD: A Guide for Parents Whose Child Is More Intense, Sensitive, Perceptive, Persistent, Energetic
by Mary Sheedy Kurcinka (HarperCollins, 1992)

Kurcinka stresses the importance of temperamental fit between parents and child. Using a positive, often humorous approach, she gives parents the tools for coping with spirited kids. The book is filled with real-life examples that will ring true for all parents.

WHEN KIDS ARE MAD, NOT BAD:
A Guide to Recognizing and Handling Children's Anger
by Henry A. Paul, M.D. (Berkley Books, 1995)

This in-depth discussion of anger explains both its causes and effects, the different forms it takes (such as depression and tantrums), how it can be expressed in healthy rather than destructive ways, and how parents can help their children work through anger rather than suppress it.

THE OPTIMISTIC CHILD
by Martin E. P. Seligman, Ph.D.
(Houghton Mifflin, 1995)

Seligman outlines a program for increasing children's optimism. Containing worksheets, cartoons, quizzes, and dialogue, it offers a plan for helping children change their pessimistic thought patterns.

ANGER: The Misunderstood Emotion
by Carol Tavris (Simon & Schuster, 1989)

Tavris takes on the myth of cathartic anger, explaining that expression of angry feelings leads to more, not less anger. Lively anecdotes help her make her very persuasive point.

NORMAL CHILDREN HAVE PROBLEMS, TOO:
How Parents Can Understand and Help
by Stanley Turecki, M.D.
(Bantam Doubleday Dell, 1995)

This book gives good information on the emotional difficulties experienced by many kids, but it's particularly helpful to parents who are asking themselves, "Does my child need professional help?"

The following classic books are out of print, but worth borrowing from your library:

MONSTERS UNDER THE BED AND OTHER CHILDHOOD FEARS
by Stephen W. Garber, Ph.D., et al.
(Villard Books, 1993)

This very readable book suggests a plan for coping with children's fears, and then catalogues childhood fears by theme. Each chapter has its own suggested reading list.

WHEN YOUR CHILD IS AFRAID
by Dr. Robert Schachter & Carole Spearin McCauley (Simon & Schuster, 1988)

Children's fears are comprehensively catalogued by age, along with strategies for allaying them. The book offers helpful ways to distinguish fears from phobias.

GAMES

EMOTIONS POSTER
(Courage to Change catalog, Tel. 800/440-4003)

This laminated, colorful poster pictures over sixty different expressions, in words and cartoon faces, and can be written on with markers. Children and parents can either circle how they feel or write their name in a box.

KIDS MAGNEPOEM—EXPRESSIONS
by Illuminations

Over 250 magnetic tiles, each with a single word, can be moved around on the refrigerator or a free-standing board to compose poems and/or stories about feelings and moods. Available at many gift stores.

THE UNGAME, KIDS VERSION
by Talicor, Inc. (Tel. 800/433-4263)

This noncompetitive game of self-expression comes with two sets of cards—one lighthearted and the other more serious—with statements and questions, such as, "Mark and Matt are good friends to each other. How would you describe a good friend?" Players take turns sharing their answers and reactions.

CASSETTE TAPES

WILL YOU BE MY FRIEND?
by The Roches

Songs for five-to seven-year-olds about disappointment, friendship, jealousy, and mean kids highlight this collection.

WISHES AND DREAMS
by Carla Sciaky (Alacazam)

This cassette explores some of the quieter feelings, like having a good day, how a rainy day feels, and what it feels like to miss a good friend.

VIDEOS

THE BERENSTAIN BEARS
(Random House, various years)

Many of the Berenstain books about feelings, (fear of the dark and of doctors, the difficulties of friendship and of sibling rivalry) are played out in these delightful animated cartoons.

BORN FREE
(1966 & TV version, 1996)

This perennially moving story of the love between researchers and a pack of lions, especially Elsa, is about the power of love and the trials of separation.

FLY AWAY HOME
(1996)

A thirteen-year-old girl and her estranged dad adopt an orphaned flock of geese and teach them, impossibly enough, to fly.

OLD YELLER
(1957)

In Texas, in the 1860s, a boy named Travis and a stray dog find each other and develop an intense bond that sees them through many adventures. A classic. ❑